POLÍTICAS

W/

D0187764

POLÍTICAS

Latina Public Officials in Texas

SONIA R. GARCÍA

VALERIE MARTINEZ-EBERS

IRASEMA CORONADO

SHARON A. NAVARRO

PATRICIA A. JARAMILLO

FOREWORD BY PATRICIA MADRID

UNIVERSITY OF TEXAS PRESS, AUSTIN

COPYRIGHT © 2008 BY THE UNIVERSITY OF TEXAS PRESS

All rights reserved

Printed in the United States of America

First edition, 2008

Requests for permission to reproduce material from this work
should be sent to Permissions, University of Texas Press,
P.O. Box 7819, Austin, TX 78713-7819
www.utexas.edu/utpress/about/bpermission.html

♾ The paper used in this book meets the minimum requirements
of ANSI/NISO Z39.48-1992 (R1997) (Permanence of Paper).

LIBRARY OF CONGRESS CATALOGING-IN-PUBLICATION DATA

Políticas : Latina public officials in Texas / Sonia R. García . . .
[et al.] ; foreword by Patricia Madrid.—1st ed.
    p.   cm.
  Includes bibliographical references and index.

ISBN 978-0-292-71788-6 (pbk. : alk. paper)
  1. Mexican American women politicians—Texas. I. García,
Sonia R. (Sonia Rebecca), 1961–
  HQ1236.5.U6P655 2008
  976.4'004680082—dc22

                            2007031377

To all the Latina trailblazers in U.S. politics, past and present

CONTENTS

FOREWORD

This book applies a gendered lens to aid in the interpretation and understanding of Latina politics. Specifically, each of the women discussed in this book offers us a glimpse of the political experience as the first ever Latina elected officials in a conservative southern state, Texas.

The authors examine the ways that gender enters into, helps to shape, and affects elections in Texas, from local city council races to statewide campaigns for public office. As all the chapters demonstrate, gender dynamics are important in the conduct and outcomes of elections. To date, Texas has yet to elect a Latina woman to the position of a U.S. representative or senator, much less governor or lieutenant governor. Nevertheless, many Latinas have run for various offices in state government. This book analyzes the support they have received, the problems they have confronted, and why there are not more of them. Women of color face additional and distinctive challenges in electoral politics because of the interaction of their race or ethnicity and gender. This book attempts to contribute to an understanding of the status of and electoral circumstances confronted by Latina women.

In many ways the experiences of these Latinas are similar to my experiences in New Mexico and in other places in the country. I am a Latina who has been involved in politics for the last twenty-five years, and I have worked to further Hispanic and women's rights all my life.

I have run five statewide campaigns, although not all of them were successful. I have knocked on thousands of doors. I have walked many miles in local parades (in high heels no less), and I have traveled every dusty road in New Mexico many times over. In 2006, I was a candidate for the U.S. Congress. It has not been an easy path. Being a Latina did not make the path any easier.

I am also a Latina who dared to run for the top law enforcement position in the state of New Mexico: attorney general, "the ultimate boy job." Being the first Latina attorney general in the history of the United States, and the first female attorney general in New Mexico's history, I have had my fair share of experience in breaking down barriers. I had no role models. I had to forge a path myself, and it often felt like being the point in a reconnaissance patrol: I was the one they were all shooting at. I found that life as attorney general was more than life in the fast lane. It was life in the oncoming lane.

What I have found most gratifying as a groundbreaker is watching the incredibly accomplished women who have come after me. I was the first woman elected to the district court bench in New Mexico, but look where we are now, twenty years later. The judiciary is filled with outstanding women at all levels. While I have been fortunate to have achieved a number of firsts, I know I am simply the first in a line of talented women.

I am a native New Mexican. I grew up in the small city of Las Cruces, in southern New Mexico, in a farming family with four brothers and two sisters. One of my sisters is a doctor, and the other, a scientist. Growing up, we had a game we played: *¿Quién es más macha?*—Who is more tough? We are a family of strong women.

My parents taught us that we could accomplish anything. Being a woman was no hindrance to what we could achieve. My father is Tiwa Indian; my mother is Hispanic. During the Civil War, soldiers came through New Mexico, so there is Irish and German in my heritage as well. By virtue of both birth and good fortune, I am multicultural. And I am fortunate to live in a state that celebrates multiculturalism. Unfortunately, I question whether my country does or not.

I believe that diversity makes America great, but I also believe that it is testing our democracy. Diversity can be a strength when it brings people together to share different perspectives, but diversity can be a weakness if it leads to cultural and—more significantly—economic divisions in our country.

Today I see the diversity in our country creating a growing economic divide that separates the rich from the poor, the black from the white, and the white from the brown. This economic division draws a sharp line between those who must decide whether they will pay their utility bill or purchase a needed prescription, and those who can afford vacations every year. This kind of economic disparity governs who is heard in the corridors of power and what color skin our leaders have.

The leaders who are heard in these corridors determine policy for the rest of America—rich and poor, brown and white alike. Until we close this economic divide and elect more leaders who look like America, we will be a nation beholden to the interests of the few.

Today we see the problems with such a system. We have a federal government that chooses the profits of corporations over the safety of our citizens and our environmental legacy. We have a federal government that reflects a narrow segment of the population. And we have a federal government that does not embrace the promise of diversity. Given the choice, I prefer my vistas to be free of drilling rigs. I prefer my air clean and my water safe to drink. I prefer diversity in wildlife as well as in our citizens. I prefer a government of the people, by the people, and for the people.

A few years ago I was on a television show with my friend Ken Salazar, then attorney general of Colorado (and now a U.S. senator). We discussed the fact that the two of us were among a handful of Hispanics in the country who had won statewide elections, not just districts that were dominated by Hispanics. As attorneys general, we were not simply token "Hispanic" elected officials. Ken and I were serving *all the people* of our states regardless of their ethnicity or political affiliation.

I am a Latina woman, but I am a New Mexican and an American leader. I embrace the diversity of my country and my state. And I believe that as we move forward and embrace the rich cultural diversity of our country, we will become stronger. Today, however, we must, as Latinas, move our country toward that future, leading by example.

I have been given a wonderful opportunity as New Mexico's first female attorney general and the nation's first Latina attorney general. I hope that I have served as a role model and inspired young women to recognize that there are no limits. Young women should aim high and let their dreams carry them as far as possible. My parents gave me a sense that anything was possible, as long as I was willing to work hard. I learned early that being a woman is no hindrance, and that is a lesson I would like all young women to learn—and live by.

This book, in many respects, reflects my experiences as a Latina leader in this country. Texas, like New Mexico, has made significant headway with regard to the number of Latinas elected to public office. But our work is not done. Young women must draw from our experiences and lessons, and continue to seek leadership positions. Latina leaders must continue to hold the torch for our communities.

Patricia Madrid
New Mexico Attorney General
July 18, 2006

PREFACE

It is especially fitting that this book on Latina trailblazers in Texas was a collaborative effort by the "first wave" of Latina political scientists to serve on the faculty of Texas universities. The project has its origins dating back to 1998, when John Bretting, a faculty member at the University of Texas–San Antonio, organized a panel of Latina political scientists for Women's History Week. At that time, we estimated there were only ten Latinas nationally with doctorates in political science, and only four in the state of Texas.

The topic of the panel focused on the trials and tribulations of being a Latina/Chicana faculty member in a political science department. The participants, all professors, were Irasema Coronado, Sonia R. García, Valerie Martinez-Ebers, and Lisa Jo Montoya. Needless to say, it was an empowering experience for all of us. After the completion of the very frank and candid panel discussions, we adjourned to several of San Antonio's historic gathering places. Dr. García, who was specializing in U.S. Latina politics, initiated conversations on the subject with all of us; these conversations rapidly turned to the notion of developing a book to recognize the "Latina firsts" in Texas. Since we were the first Latina political scientists in Texas, it made absolute sense to write about Latina leaders in the political arena, specifically from Texas.

This book is the ultimate result of these earlier conversations. The turning point was in September 2003 at a conference in San Antonio of Mujeres Activas en Letras y Cambio Social (MALCS), a scholarly meeting of Latina academics and activists. Dr. García attended a presentation sponsored by the University of Texas Press regarding the nuts and bolts of submitting book manuscripts. The information helped tremendously because the book proposal was accepted almost immediately after it was submitted.

Things have changed since 1998. Lisa Jo Montoya left the discipline for the life of a political consultant. Valerie Martinez-Ebers is a tenured faculty member at Texas Christian University in Fort Worth, and became the first Latina president of the Western Political Science Association. Sonia García is also a tenured faculty member; she serves as department chair and graduate director of the Department of Political Science at St. Mary's University in San Antonio. Irasema Coronado finished her Ph.D. at the University of Arizona and ultimately returned to the Mexico/U.S. borderlands, where she is an associate professor of political science at the University of Texas–El Paso and associate dean for the College of Liberal Arts. Three of the four original Latina scholars remain in this collaborative project. Two additional Latina political scientists from Texas were brought on board. Sharon A. Navarro and Patricia Jaramillo were both new faculty members and the first Latinas at the University of Texas–San Antonio in the Political Science Department when they joined our project.

We estimate that there are now seven Latina political scientists teaching at Texas universities. Latinas still make up less than 2 percent of those with Ph.D. degrees in political science. We want to recognize the first Latinas to earn a Ph.D. in the field of political science: Professors Adaljiza Sosa-Riddle, Debra Salazar, Velma Garcia, and Christine M. Sierra. We hope this book will inspire future graduate students and academics, especially Latinas, to study political science and continue this important research. We especially hope we can recruit more Latinas to join us on our very challenging journey!

ACKNOWLEDGMENTS

Our project would not have been possible were it not for the willingness of the Latinas in this book to share their stories. We are truly inspired by their courage and successes. We hope they will also inspire our readers, especially young Latinas, to consider a profession in public service. We would also like to thank New Mexico's attorney general, Patricia Madrid, for writing the book's foreword. We had the opportunity to meet her at a scholarly conference in Albuquerque in 2006 during her campaign for the U.S. Congress. Similar to the women in this book, she is a trailblazer in many respects.

This book would not have been possible without the assistance of several individuals. First, we wish to acknowledge the efforts of Professor John Bretting, currently at the University of Texas–El Paso, for his pivotal role in bringing us together and inspiring this project, as well as his continued encouragement to bring it to fruition. We also want to acknowledge Theresa May at the University of Texas Press for her faith in the project. We also want to express our gratitude to the reviewers of the manuscript— Carol Hardy-Fanta, Luis Fraga, and Lisa Magaña—for their helpful suggestions and insightful comments.

There are other colleagues who read drafts of our manuscript that we would like to thank, including Dr. Kathleen Staudt from the University of Texas–El Paso; Dr. Marisela Márquez, an administrator from the University of California–Santa Barbara; Dr. Christine Brenner from Rutgers University–Camden; and Dr. Kamala Platt.

Many students and administrative staff were also instrumental in this project. We would like to thank graduate students Jessica Ramos and Rick

Vela from St. Mary's University, as well as Mona Segura, Leandro Salazar, Jonatan Paredes, Anne Crowther, and Daniel Martinez from the University of Texas–El Paso.

Finally, we would like to give special thanks to the individuals in our personal lives who have supported us throughout this venture. These include Charley García; Cary, Gabriel, and Maria Patricia Reeves; Vidal and Hope R. Navarro; Leslie Navarro-Davis; Faith Perez and Roberto Perez-diaz; and Scott and Nate Ebers.

We hope that this book educates young people about important Latina women in Texas, provides a source of inspiration for those who aspire to public service, and pays tribute to all the Latinas who have made history.

POLÍTICAS

CHAPTER 1

UNDERSTANDING LATINA POLITICAL LEADERSHIP

Latinas,[1] especially those of Mexican descent, have a long history as political actors dating at least as far back as the Texas revolution in 1836, when Francisca Alvarez, the so-called "Angel of Goliad," persuaded Mexican officers to defy the execution orders given by their president, General Antonio López de Santa Anna, thus saving the lives of numerous Texas soldiers held as prisoners of war. Since 1959, when Norma Zuniga Benavides successfully ran for school board trustee in Laredo, Texas, Latinas have served in public office in the United States (Cotera 1976; Gomez-Quiñones 1990; Acosta and Winegarten 2003). Only recently, however, have scholars begun to examine the complexity and contributions of Latina leadership in the American political context.

What motivates Latinas to become involved in political activity, and what barriers do they confront in their efforts? Do they typically follow the conventional paths of men and women of other races and ethnic groups? As elected leaders, do they have unique political perspectives and/or skills gleaned from their cultural background or life experiences? Finally, how does their leadership influence public policy? To answer these central questions, this book presents case studies of the first elected and appointed Latina public officials in various levels of offices in the state of Texas. Specifically, we describe and analyze the political stories of women who have reached public office as the "first state legislator," the "first state senator," the "first mayor of a major Texas city," and so on.

These detail-rich case studies, derived primarily from personal interviews, are intended to provide readers with a multidimensional understanding of Latinas' political leadership. As Alessandro Portelli, a leading scholar utilizing oral history, explains, "Oral sources tell us not just what people did, but what they wanted to do, what they believed they were doing and what they now think they did" (in Stille 2001). As much as possible, we substantiate their subjective stories with archival data and other sources. We also examine and compare these stories in light of conclusions drawn from earlier studies of women in politics. Our methods make these case studies both descriptive and theory-building.

Undoubtedly, the numbers and influence of Latina political leaders are increasing at the national level and in states other than Texas. However, taking a case study approach within one state is a first step towards fully understanding the efforts and impacts of Latina public officials. It is our hope that future research will continue our approach by examining Latina leadership in other states.

Examining the first Latinas elected to specific positions in Texas has important implications. First of all, since Latinas are underrepresented, these first Latina public officials have already paid a price in crossing the barriers to their entry into politics; pressure is increased when she is the first one, or the only one, because of society's tendency to stereotype her as representative of all Latinas. Second, Texas leads the country with respect to the largest number of Latinas (and Latinos) elected to public office. Third, as the demographic makeup of the state and the country changes, we all benefit from understanding how an inclusive and diverse democracy should work. Fourth, with the 2000 Census pronouncement of Latinos as the largest ethnic group in the United States, we can expect that this population will continue to seek political representation at all levels of government. With that as a given, it is essential to examine Latinas, specifically Mexican American women, and their role in politics.

NATIONAL ATTENTION TO LATINAS

Events prompting this study of Latina trailblazers started in the late 1980s, when Latinas achieved a new presence and level of visibility in the national political arena. Ileana Ros-Lehtinen (R-FL), a Cuban American, received national attention in 1982 as the first Latina to be elected to the U.S. Congress. Ten years later, in 1992, two additional Latinas were elected to the U.S. House of Representatives: Lucille Roybal-Allard (D-CA), the first Mexican American representative from California, and Nydia Velásquez (D-NY), the first Puerto Rican representative from New York.

In 1996, Loretta Sánchez, a businesswoman from Orange County, California, brought further public attention as well as notoriety to Latinas in

politics when she narrowly defeated Republican incumbent Robert Dornan in a bitterly fought election. The controversial longtime incumbent
Dornan was targeted as "out of touch" with his constituency, especially
after a distracting run for the 1996 Republican presidential nomination.
The 46th District had always had a slight Democratic majority, but it
became even more Democratic after the 1990 Census, which showed a
considerable increase in Hispanics living in the district. Sánchez won by
only 984 votes on the strength of support from Hispanics and blue-collar
workers. Dornan contested the election, alleging that some of the registered voters were not U.S. citizens, but the results were upheld. Sánchez
handily defeated Dornan in a 1998 rematch and has not since faced serious
opposition.

In a short period of time, three other Latina Democrats were sent to
the U.S. House from California: former state legislator Grace Napolitano
(1998), former state senator Hilda Solis (2000), and lawyer and activist
Linda Sánchez (2003), the sister of Loretta Sánchez. The Sánchez sisters
received national acclaim as the first "sister act" in the Congress. As of
2006, seven Latinas were serving in Congress, all in the House of Representatives. No Latina has ever run for or been elected to the U.S. Senate.
In 2006 Patricia Madrid, attorney general of New Mexico, ran for Congress
in one of the most competitive races for the Democratic Party nationwide,
hoping to be the first Latina congresswoman from New Mexico. U.S. Representative Heather Wilson (R) edged out Madrid by 879 votes.[2]

Although numerous Latinas have sought Texas congressional seats, the
Lone Star State has yet to elect a Latina to the thirty-two-member delegation to the U.S. Congress. Two prominent Latinas ran in Texas Democratic primaries in 1996 for the House of Representatives: Dolores Briones,
who was elected as county judge in 1998, campaigned unsuccessfully for
an open seat in El Paso, while Mary Helen Berlanga, the first Latina on
the State Board of Education, unsuccessfully challenged the incumbent
in Corpus Christi on the Gulf Coast. Four years later, Latinas tried again.
Although attorney and community activist Diana Rivera-Martinez unsuccessfully challenged the incumbent in the Democratic primary in Mer-
cedes in south Texas, Regina Montoya Coggins won the Democratic nomination in Dallas, but was unsuccessful in her bid to unseat the Republican
incumbent in the general election.

Other more recent, albeit unsuccessful, stories regarding Latina congressional candidates are demonstrative of their continuing emergence.
These candidacies are also indicative of the tough challenges these
women face in the Lone Star State. In 2004, state judge Leticia Hinojosa

from McAllen unsuccessfully challenged incumbent Lloyd Doggett in the Democratic primary in the newly constructed 25th Congressional District, which stretches more than 350 miles from Austin to McAllen. Some would argue that the new configuration was intentionally designed by the Republican majority in the state legislature to defeat Representative Doggett. Interestingly, the former chair of the Texas Public Utilities Commission, Rebecca Armendariz Klein, won the Republican nomination but could not defeat Doggett in the restructured district. In another newly restructured district, Houston businesswoman and attorney Arlette Molina won the Republican primary but was unable to defeat the Democratic challenger, Al Green, a former justice of the peace and president of the local NAACP chapter.

Texas Latinas, like Latinas nationwide, are notably more successful in winning elections for state legislative seats.[3] For example, Polly Baca-Barragan was the first Latina elected to both the Colorado House of Representatives and the Colorado Senate, in 1974 and 1978, respectively. The first Latina ever elected to a state legislature in the United States, Baca-Barragan served for twelve years. She also was the first Latina to be nominated by a major political party for the U.S. House of Representatives, in 1980, and the first Latina to serve in a state party leadership role (Senate Democratic Caucus), in 1985–1986. Other significant Latina firsts include the late Texas state representative Irma Rangel, who was first elected in 1976 and served fourteen consecutive terms prior to her death in 2003.

Gloria Molina was California's first Latina state legislator, elected in 1982. She resigned in 1987 and successfully ran for the Los Angeles City Council. In 1991, Molina became the first Mexican American of either sex to be elected to the Los Angeles County Board of Supervisors. As the first Latina on the board, Molina was also the first Latina elected to local office to receive national publicity.

The increasing number of Latina candidates in hotly contested elections at county, city, and school district levels in prominent urban areas such as San Francisco and Pasadena, California; Phoenix, Arizona; San Antonio, Houston, and Dallas, Texas; and Santa Fe, New Mexico, has continued to focus national media attention on the importance of Latina leadership in local arenas.

Interestingly, from our perspective as Texas scholars, a local Latina leader making national news in 2004 was Dallas County sheriff Lupe Valdez. A retired federal law enforcement officer, Valdez outpolled three opponents in the 2004 Democratic primary and then went on to narrowly defeat the Republican challenger, a thirty-year veteran of the Sheriff's Department. It is important to note that Valdez is making history as the first woman, the first Hispanic, and the first openly gay person to serve in this capacity (Moreno 2004).

PATTERNS OF REPRESENTATION FOR LATINAS

Although Latinas have made gains in politics in recent years, there are still relatively few in office, and for the most part they are unrecognized as political actors. Since the 1980s, many organizations and scholars have tracked the level of political involvement of Latinos and Latinas. According to the National Association for Latino Elected and Appointed Officials (NALEO), there were 3,128 Latino/a elected officials nationwide in 1984, 4,625 in 1994, and ten years later that number had risen to 5,041. As of 2005, there were more than 6,000 elected and appointed Latino/a officials, an almost 100 percent increase in representation over the past twenty years.[4]

As the importance of gender in electoral politics increased, greater scholarly attention was given to disaggregating Latino and Latina elected officials.[5] Sierra and Sosa-Riddell (1994) reported 592 Latina elected officials in 1987, and that total increased to 744 in 1989. By 1992, Latinas comprised more than 30 percent of all Latino/a elected officials, when women as a whole constituted only 17.2 percent of all elected officials in the country. Significantly, Latina officials were most prominent on local school boards and in municipal governments (Pachon and DeSipio 1992, cited in Montoya et al. 2000).

As of 2004, Latinas held 27.4 percent of all elected positions held by Latinos and Latinas nationwide, a slight drop in their relative proportion, but Latinas had the highest representation in state senates of all Latino/a elected officials (40 percent), followed by 33 percent in county offices, 32 percent in Congress, 32 percent on school boards, 26 percent in state houses, 24 percent in municipal offices, and 23 percent in judicial/law enforcement offices. One study, covering 1990 to 2002, shows that Latinas made significant progress in the Congress (from one to seven representatives) and in state offices (increasing from sixteen to sixty-one). Latina increases still outpaced increases in Latino/a representation overall, as well as increases among white women (Fraga and Navarro 2004).

Regarding Latina representation in Texas, in 1991 Texas led all other states with significant Hispanic populations, with 361 Latina elected officials, followed by California (163) and New Mexico (135). By 1999, Texas led the country in the total number of Latinos elected to public office, but when the numbers were disaggregated by gender, Texas ranked only sixth out of the states with significant Hispanic populations. Arizona and California—followed by Florida, Colorado, and New York—ranked above Texas.[6] In 2005, NALEO reported that there were 2,137 Latino elected officials in Texas, 591 of them (over 30 percent) women. As mentioned above, Texas Latinas once again rank first in the country in the number of public officials, followed by California, New Mexico, Arizona, and Colorado. The majority of Texas Latina elected officials can be found in municipal and county offices and on school boards.

THE STATUS OF U.S. LATINAS

To fully understand the significance of Latinas achieving some prominence in elected office, it is necessary to acknowledge the struggles that U.S. Latinas have faced and continue to face. Research in history and the social sciences has documented and illustrated the discrimination and oppression experienced by Mexican American women (Melville 1980; Cordova et al. 1986). These early studies underscore the complexity of Latinas' experiences in the United States. A growing area of research addresses the legal issues faced by and impacting Mexican American women and Latinas in general (Hernandez 1976; Ontiveros 1993; Valencia et al. 2004). The host of issues affecting Latinas range from reproductive rights, pregnancy discrimination, workplace discrimination, equal pay, educational attainment, and affirmative action to sexual harassment, domestic violence, and sexual violence. Mexican American women have played a pivotal role in the struggle for equality and justice for Latinos. Organizations such as Comisión Femeníl Mexicana Nacional (established in 1973), the Mexican American Legal Defense and Education Fund (MALDEF) Chicana Rights Project (established in 1974), and other women's legal organizations played key roles in bringing cases in the courts (Valencia et al. 2004, 41).

With regard to reproductive rights, "the issue of voluntary consent for sterilization is an area of particular relevance" to Latinas (Valencia 2004, 43). In *Madrigal v. Quilligan* (1981), a federal court in California heard a challenge by Mexican and Mexican American women who alleged that the University of Southern California, Los Angeles County Medical Center performed illegal and unwanted sterilizations upon them without their consent (ibid.). Although the trial court in *Madrigal* denied the women's claims, reasoning that the sterilizations resulted because of the women's limited English abilities and their "cultural background," the case resulted in stricter federal regulations requiring medical consent in one's native language.

With regard to workplace discrimination, Valencia and colleagues also point out how the challenges that all women face are compounded for Latinas, especially "when one considers the intersection of various factors, including gender, race and ethnicity, class, language ability, and immigrant status" (2004, 48). As a result of the cumulative effect of these factors, Latinas are more likely to work in traditionally segregated jobs, as secretaries, custodians, maids, nannies, and garment workers. They are also more likely to be the lowest paid workers in comparison to men and other related groups of women. The U.S. Department of Labor and the U.S. Equal Employment Opportunity Commission reported in 1999 that while women earn only seventy-five cents for every dollar that a man earns, African American women earn just sixty-five cents, and Hispanic women earn fifty-five cents for each dollar that white men earn.

In addition, given the realities of the country's segregated workforce, Latino/a undocumented immigrants, legal residents, and U.S. citizens often work side by side. In *EEOC v. Tortilleria La Mejor* (1991), the Equal Employment Opportunity Commission and a Latina plaintiff "successfully argued in federal court that the protections under Title VII of the Civil Rights Act of 1964 were applicable to all workers irrespective of their legal status" (Valencia et al. 2004, 49). Earlier, Mexicans and Mexican Americans who worked as maids in a hotel in California successfully challenged the discrimination and sexual harassment they faced in federal court in the 1989 case *EEOC v. Hacienda Hotel*.

In sum, Latinas have been at the forefront of legal battles in the fight for equality and justice for Mexican American women—and for all women. Latinas "have had to struggle with the dual challenge of being both Mexican American and female" (Valencia et al. 2004, 61). The intersection of these two forces means that they, and Latinas in general, face unique issues, as in the realm of reproductive rights and workplace discrimination.

LATINA ORGANIZATIONS

One factor contributing to the increased political representation of Latinas is the early involvement and support of Latina organizations. In many cases, Latinas in political office received their initial training from community-based organizations and activities (Takash-Cruz 1993; Hardy-Fanta 1993; Prindeville 2002). One recent study shows how Latinas, like women from other races and ethnic groups, are creating their own paths of leadership development and advocacy by forming various Latina-based organizations (García and Márquez 2005). National organizations that have helped to prepare Latina women for political office include the League of United Latin American Citizens (LULAC) Ladies Auxiliary, which established chapters as early as the 1930s; the Mexican American National Association (MANA), established in 1974; and Comisión Femenil Mexicana Nacional, established in 1973. Other Latino/a-based organizations established in the 1970s and 1980s—such as the National Hispana Leadership Institute, MALDEF, and Southwest Voter Registration and Education Project (SWVREP)—offer leadership training for Latinos in politics. Similarly, the National Women's Political Caucus (NWPC), established in 1971, and specifically the Hispanic Steering Committee have sponsored candidate development conferences for Latinas, and NWPC currently provides resources for female candidates of color. Regional organizations established in the 1980s and 1990s also target and assist potential political candidates; the Hispanic Women's Political Coalition in Denver, Colorado; the Hispanic Women in Leadership in Houston, Texas; and Hispanas Organized for Political Empowerment in California are a few examples.

Political action committees have also been formed to foster Latinas running for office. Although technically not a formal political action committee, the Latina Political Action Committee (LPAC) (established in the mid-1980s and based in Sacramento, California) was formed to elect more Latinas and raise money for Latina candidates. Formal PACs such as the Florida Hispanic Women's Pact and the Latina P.A.C. in Houston raise money for Latina candidates and others who support their issues. Latina P.A.C., in particular, established in 1991, supports qualified Latina candidates for elected and appointed positions, regardless of political affiliation.

LATINAS IN TEXAS

Given this book's focus on Latinas in Texas politics, a review of their political role in a historical context is necessary. Generally speaking, Texas women in the 1990s experienced less than average status compared to women in the other forty-nine states. Studies show that Texas ranked thirtieth in terms of the number of women in the state legislature in 1996. A report on the status of women in Texas by the Institute for Women's Policy Research indicates that Texas ranked seventeenth in the nation in terms of the number of women elected to state and national offices in 2000.[7]

Mexican American women have served in various public offices (Acosta and Winegarten 2003). As mentioned earlier, since 1959 Mexican American women have served in elected positions. Research also documents

Mexican American women's involvement in securing women's right to vote in the 1900s, and in forming *mutualistas*, or mutual aid societies, beginning in the 1920s. These societies were informal networks that provided assistance and services to recent Mexican immigrants. Mexican American women were also involved in the Chicano civil rights movement and the women's movement during the 1960s and 1970s. They have been involved in party politics, registering voters and collecting poll taxes, and during the 1960s, many were involved in Viva Kennedy Clubs. Some women formed organizations within the two major parties: the Mexican American Democrats (MAD) (later the Tejano Democrats) and the Mexican American Republicans of Texas (MART). Many women also got involved in third party politics, specifically La Raza Unida in the 1960s and 1970s. In many cases, Chicanas ran for public office as La Raza Unida candidates. As early as 1964, Virginia Muzquiz did so, running for the Texas state legislature. Likewise, Tejana candidates Alma Canales and Marta Cotera ran for statewide offices in 1972.

Latinas have also been involved in other political organizations, such as the American GI Forum Women's Auxiliary, the Political Association of Spanish-speaking Organizations (PASSO), and the Texas Women's Political Caucus. These groups and the women associated with them often helped launch Tejanas' ascension to public office (Acosta and Winegarten 2003).

THEORETICAL FRAMEWORK

Although Latinas have gained visibility in the national political arena and have clearly demonstrated leadership in U.S. politics, very few studies document their significance and potential as elected officials. Latina scholars have begun to fill the void in this area of research. Sierra and Sosa-Riddell contend that "Latina activity is highly complex and comprised of many diverse forms of political practice and intervention" (1994, 307). Motivated by the desire to solve problems in their neighborhoods, schools, and communities, Latinas are more likely to be active in grassroots political organizing. However, some Latinas have a more general commitment to the notion of public service, a motivation that leads them to activities in electoral politics. Political participation is typically viewed as being divided into two separate spheres, electoral and grassroots, and political scholars often confine their research to a single sphere. Latina leaders, however, frequently remain active or at least maintain connections in both spheres simultaneously (Sierra and Sosa-Riddell 1994; Pardo 1990; Takash-Cruz

1993; Montoya et al. 2000; García and Márquez 2001). We expect to find evidence of this interconnectedness and overlapping activity among the Latinas in our study.

The sense of a strong Mexican cultural identity, with its traditions and ties to religion and spirituality, is also important to Latinas in politics. Because of this strong connection to their culture, Latinas are also likely to retain their traditional gender roles while advocating for their community. The literature on Chicana feminism suggests that Latinas do not separate politics from the needs of the family and the Latino community as a whole (Pesquera and Segura 1993). Perhaps due to family responsibilities and traditional cultural sex roles, Latinas are more likely to develop policy priorities and direct their activities to the needs of women and families, and their particular ethnic communities. These important elements of their political socialization and orientations are shaped by their unique experiences and political history as minority women (García and Márquez 2001). Thus, we expect the Latinas in our study to demonstrate a strong cultural identity as well as a focus or emphasis on policies that assist families and Latino communities.

Some scholars of race/ethnicity politics find that Latinas demonstrate "a vision of politics" that is more participatory or inclusive (Hardy-Fanta 1993). Latinas are also able to transform traditional networks, resources, and relationships based on family and culture and use them as political assets (Pardo 1990). Equally important, Latinas demonstrate a capacity to overcome barriers of race, class, gender, and culture largely because they are able to draw from their experiences as longtime community activists (Takash-Cruz 1993; Sierra 1997; García and Márquez 2001).

Research also addresses how Latinas are politically motivated by various reasons, incentives that combine traditionally relevant, political goals with specific community-oriented objectives (García and Márquez 2001). They exhibit a commitment to getting particular candidates elected and certain policies addressed, as well as a commitment to their individual communities (influenced by the demographic makeup of the district or city) and the Chicano/Latino community at large. Latinas manifest abilities to bridge traditional and community motivations for their political involvement (García and Márquez 2001). As they enter traditional mainstream politics, Latinas bring with them their experiences from grassroots politics and from cultural networks and resources (García and Márquez 2001). Similarly, we expect that the Latinas in our study will demonstrate these attitudinal characteristics, as well as draw from their families and cultural networks.

Finally, recent scholarship theorizes that Latinas are well positioned as powerbrokers and have the potential to play key roles in American politics. Given their multiple identities as women, women of color, members of an ethnic minority, and part of a growing immigrant constituency, Latinas have a unique perspective and ability to advocate for multiple constituencies as well as adapt to different contexts (Fraga et al. 2005; Fraga and Navarro 2004). This intersectionality of identities provides Latinas with resources and skills to negotiate and form coalitions. In particular, they have the capacity to bridge the barriers between women of different ethnic and racial groups, as well as between men and women of different racial and ethnic groups. Similarly, we expect to find that the Latinas in our study demonstrate the capacity to negotiate, form coalitions, and adapt to differing political contexts.

Although Latinas share certain experiences as women of color, it is also important to note that they are not homogenous. There are various differences among Latina candidates and public officials that are based on many factors. Some of these cleavages are common among all people in politics, such as educational levels, class, ideological differences, feminist orientations, religion, partisanship, marital status, gender, motherhood, and sexuality. Other differences, however, impact Latinos and Latinas specifically, such as language, immigrant status, ancestry, cultural orientations, degree of assimilation, historical experiences, and regional backgrounds. These differences highlight the importance of coalitions and compromise within the larger Latino community. Coalitions are especially important today, given the increasing concern for immigrant rights within the Latino community.

A related point is that in most other contexts, the ability to advocate for multiple constituencies may not be viewed positively. Representatives that advocate for multiple groups may be viewed as not being loyal, as "flip-flopping," or as "sitting on a fence." However, in electoral politics, given the dynamics and necessity of compromise and coalitions, advocating with an understanding of multiple constituencies should be considered a unique strength. Democratic theory suggests that politics centers on conflict, compromise, cooperation, and coalitions. Effective representatives need certain skills, including the ability to form coalitions and mobilize communities, to negotiate differences, and to view politics as inclusive and participatory. The strategies that Latinas employ provide an excellent model to broaden our understanding of U.S. electoral politics.

FORMAT AND AREAS OF INQUIRY

As mentioned, this book provides case studies of the first elected and appointed Latina public officials in Texas, and it is dedicated to Latinas in statewide office, in the Texas State House, and in the Texas Senate, and to those who are judges, city mayors, and city council members. With regard to municipal offices, Latinas were selected by city, based on the city's size or historical significance. It is important to note that, although it is beyond the scope of this particular project, the authors recognize that many Latinas hold county positions in Texas.

The objectives of the book are as follows: 1) to present an overview of Latinas' participation in electoral politics; 2) to provide case studies of specific Latina public officials in Texas; 3) to contribute to a theoretical framework on Latina politics; and 4) to provide a basis of useful information and resources on Latinas in public office for students, practitioners of electoral politics, and aspiring public officials.

Given that the women presented in this book are the first Latinas to hold a particular office, it is essential to understand their backgrounds and initiation into politics, as well as their ascendance to public office. Four areas of inquiry bring us a step closer to understanding why there are so few: 1) political socialization; 2) the initial decision to seek public office and the experiences and barriers faced; 3) leadership style; and 4) perceptions of representational roles and advocacy priorities.

The areas addressed in the book are in some respects relevant to all public officials, to all female elected officials, and all minority public officials. However, we believe that Mexican American women as public officials, particularly "the first ones" appointed or elected to specific public offices, have unique perspectives and/or experiences. Identifying their perspectives and sharing their experiences will provide readers with a broader understanding of American politics, civic participation, and electoral politics.

With respect to political socialization, several key questions are examined. What factors influenced the socialization of the Latinas in our study? Were they raised in political families, or did they experience political socialization as adults? How does culture influence Latinas' socialization? Some of the literature on Latinas' political socialization suggests that Latinas are influenced by traditional gender roles similar to those of women in other race or ethnic groups, but they are also affected by cultural traditions that may impede or enhance political participation (Hardy-Fanta 1997; Pardo 1990).

Regarding these women's bids for public office, some of the questions include: How did they decide whether or not to run for public office? What factors do they consider in deciding whether or not to run for public office? And, how do they run their campaigns? Latinas tend to link individuals, family, friendship networks, and community relationships when running for public office (Hardy-Fanta 1993). The literature also suggests that Latinas manifest a unique form of campaigning—one that is more personal (Hardy-Fanta 1993). Gender, context, and political resources play a role in shaping the organization, message, and style of the campaigns (García and Berberena 2004).

Other questions center on the routes these women took to holding office. Do Latinas follow the same paths to office as other elected officials? The literature suggests that Latinas do not follow conventional routes. The informal requirements for elective office are usually a college education and high-status occupation, which Latinas, in general, may not have, perhaps because of deliberate and systematic discrimination. Instead, Latinas gain their political experience from community activism and participation in political campaigns (Takash-Cruz 1993; Sierra 1997; Fraga et al. 2003). Equally important is the relationship between their early political socialization and the decision to seek public office.

Related to this area of running for office are the potential obstacles for Latina candidates. The literature suggests that Latinas face barriers based on race, class, and gender (Takash-Cruz 1993; Gutiérrez and Deen 2000; García and Márquez 2001), and also that Latina public officials are able to overcome these barriers (Takash-Cruz 1993; García and Márquez 2001), including the media stereotype of Latinas as political novices. Other important challenges Latinas face are cultural and societal factors that demand traditional familial responsibilities.

The third and fourth areas of inquiry relate to leadership, advocacy, and types of representation. Do Latinas make a difference after they are elected? As leaders? As representatives of Latinas and the larger Latino community? The literature suggests that Latinas demonstrate an ability to advocate for gendered agendas and Latino-based agendas. Among their strengths is the ability to use their experiences as women and as Mexican Americans to build coalitions, and to advocate for multiple interests simultaneously (Fraga et al. 2003; Fraga and Navarro 2004).

Equally important to these areas of inquiry is demonstration of the significance of increased Latina representation. Why is it important to have more Latinas in office? Many would argue that the reason we would want more Latinas in public office is to advocate for the issues that most affect Latinas and the larger Latino community. Issues such as child care, equal pay, domestic violence, breast cancer research, and reproductive rights affect women generally, but affect women of color in different ways. Latinas clearly play a role in representing and advocating for their communities.

Electing more Latinas also brings this country closer to a true representative democracy.

METHODOLOGY

Using interviews and secondary sources, we adopted a case study approach in order to compare the experiences of the first Latinas to hold select public offices in the Texas. When possible, we conducted face-to-face and follow-up interviews with each officeholder to gain a deeper understanding of her experience. In some cases, we also interviewed staff or family members. We compiled questions for the initial interview instrument (Appendix B), recognizing that collection methods might vary according to each coauthor's interview technique. The questions focused on each woman's political biography, her personal successes as a public official, her leadership style, and her attitude regarding specific policy issues related to Latinos, such as civil rights, women's rights, and education, among others. The secondary information was obtained from newspapers and other sources.

The case studies were selected on the basis that each was the first Latina elected or appointed to that particular public office. Latinas in state, as opposed to local, offices were more clearly identifiable. Irma Rangel (Chapter 3) was selected because she was the first Latina to be elected to the Texas House of Representatives. Judith Zaffirini (Chapter 4) was selected because of her position as the first of two Latinas elected to the Texas Senate. Leticia Van de Putte (Chapter 4), the second Latina elected to the state Senate, gained additional recognition as the first Latina to serve in a party leadership role when she was selected to preside over the Democratic Caucus in the state senate. Lena Guerrero (Chapter 5) was selected because of her accomplishment as the first and only Latina to serve in a statewide office in Texas.

Chapter 6 focuses on four state judges. Texas has a three-tier judicial structure, with judges elected in partisan elections. Although no Latina has ever been elected for the highest courts (Texas has two high courts), two were selected because they serve as the first appellate justice (Linda Yañes) and first chief justice (Alma López) to serve on an appellate court. Two other Latina judges were selected for our study; the first district court judge, Elma Salinas Ender, who was initially appointed, and Mary Roman, the first Latina district court judge to be elected in a major city (San Antonio).

The selection of case studies of city council members and mayors for Chapters 7 and 8 was more pointed. We began by identifying Latinas in medium to large cities and then added cases from cities with some geographic or historical significance. The first Latina mayor of Brownsville, Blanca Sánchez Vela, and the first Latina mayor of Laredo, Betty Flores, were selected not only because they represent major cities, but because these cities are located on the Texas-Mexico border. Olivia Serna, the first Latina mayor of Crystal City, was selected because of the town's historical significance for the Chicano civil rights movement. The five case studies of the first Latinas to serve on city councils were selected because they represent medium to large cities: San Antonio, El Paso, Dallas, Houston, and Laredo.

Recognizing the similar outcomes of each case study, our investigation is concerned with how these Latinas became the first in their positions—under "what conditions (and through what paths)" (George and Bennett 2005, 78). Our selection was deliberate. Given the absence of literature on our specific questions, we decided to focus on Latinas in public office. As some of the first to attempt to address this research question, we believe this study falls under what George and Bennett describe as "the early stages of a research program," justifying selection on the dependent variable since the comparisons may still "serve the heuristic purpose of identifying the potential causal paths and variables leading to the dependent variable of interest" (2005, 23).

However, our study was also able to achieve some level of theory-testing. Drawn from an array of scholarly work, the literature can inform a set of expectations to be examined across cases. Therefore, a cross-case comparison reveals patterns that achieve a modest level of analytical rigor while also providing for the depth of each Latina's experience and the flexibility of theory-building.

We fully recognize the limitations of our research design. Our decision to use a case study approach allowed us to delve more deeply into the lives of each of our cases. However, our conclusions are thus limited to these individual women. Although we are unable to generalize to all Latina public officials, or even Latina public officials in Texas, we believe our study will encourage others to pursue other methods to further this research agenda.

OUTLINE OF BOOK

Chapter 2 presents an overview of the relevant research on Latina politics and women and politics, as well as culture, gender, and ethnicity in Texas politics. Chapter 3 is devoted to the late Irma Rangel; as the first Latina elected to the state legislature and the first in the country, her legacy will never be forgotten. Chapter 4 is dedicated to the first and only Latinas in the Texas Senate; Judith Zaffirini was first elected state senator, and Leticia Van de Putte was the first Latina selected to chair the Democratic Caucus in the senate. Chapter 5, "Latinas in Statewide Office," focuses on Lena Guerrero as the first Latina appointed to serve in a statewide office, that of railroad commissioner. Despite her political downfall, her success as an elected official and railroad commissioner cannot be ignored. Chapter 6, "Latinas on the Bench," is dedicated to the first Latina state judges. Four, in particular, are investigated: the first Latina appointed state judge, Elma Salinas Ender; the first Latina elected state judge from a major metropolitan city, Mary Roman; the first Latina appointed appellate state judge, Linda Yañes; and the first chief justice of an appellate court, Alma López. Chapter 7, "Latinas as Mayors," highlights the first Latina mayors of Laredo, Brownsville, and Crystal City, Texas. Betty Flores was elected mayor of Laredo in 1998; Blanca Sánchez Vela was elected mayor of Brownsville in 1999; and Olivia Serna was first elected by the city council as mayor of Crystal City in 1979. Chapter 8, "Latinas as City Council Members," is dedicated to the first Latina city council members from five cities. The five women whose political trajectories will be discussed are Anita Nanez Martinez, from Dallas; Alicia Chacón, from El Paso; Maria Berriozábal, from San Antonio; Graciela (Gracie) Saenz, a native of Houston; and Consuelo (Chelo) Montalvo of Laredo. The epilogue highlights some of our findings and addresses future areas of research.

CHAPTER 2

AREAS OF INQUIRY: WHY SO FEW LATINAS HOLD PUBLIC OFFICE

As discussed in Chapter 1, Latinas have gained visibility in the U.S. political arena and have clearly demonstrated leadership in national politics. However, very few studies document their importance and potential as elected officials. With the exception of those in certain offices, Latinas in politics are typically invisible in the media and academia. Part of the reason is that, generally speaking, Latinas are not considered the norm in American politics. They are not in the theoretical frameworks or paradigms in the mainstream literature on electoral politics, gender politics, or Latino politics. Also, Latina candidates and public officials are often stereotyped as passive and meek political novices. Academic research is necessary to dispel the notions that Latinas are not serious political actors, that they are inexperienced, and that they are too naïve to the necessary calculus when running for office (Hardy-Fanta 1997; García and Márquez 2001; Fraga et al. 2005).

As stated in Chapter 1, the studies starting to fill the void in this area of research highlight the complexity of Latina politics and the need for additional research (Sierra and Sosa-Riddell 1994; Montoya et al. 2000). Scholars argue that part of the problem is that researchers often divide Latina political participation into electoral political and grassroots political organizing, which ignores the interconnectedness of the two forms of activity for Latina political participation (Hardy-Fanta 1993; Takash-Cruz 1993; Sierra and Sosa-Riddell 1994; Pardo 1998; Montoya et al. 2000; García and Márquez 2001; Prindeville 2002). Equally important, because the activities of Latinas tend not to be gender-specific, their activism is not included in the broader analysis of women's activism. According to Sierra and Sosa-Riddell (1994), the goal of the literature on Latina politics is to expand "what is political" and recognize the academic inquiry of community-based organizations, labor union activity, and grassroots mobilizations as well as electoral politics.

The existing literature on Latina politics, along with mainstream literature and that on gender politics, provides useful insights into the dynamics faced by Latinas as candidates and public officials. The literature also informs our expectations for the case study analysis in the chapters that follow. We address the literature according to the four areas of inquiry introduced in Chapter 1: 1) political socialization, 2) the decision to run for office and overcoming barriers, 3) leadership, and 4) advocacy and representation. We seek to advance our knowledge of the complexity of Latinas, specifically the intersectionality of gender and ethnicity in politics, by examining the experiences of some of the first Latinas to hold public office in Texas. The literature guided our expectations in addressing these areas of inquiry: How did these Latinas become politically socialized? What motivated their decisions to seek public office? What were their experiences as leaders, advocates, and representatives? How did they view their roles in political office?

POLITICAL SOCIALIZATION

Due to the limited research on Latinas in formal political roles as elected and appointed officials, we begin our inquiry into the lives of the Latinas in our study by seeking to understand their politicization. Research consistently finds gender differences in political socialization despite the advent and aftermath of feminism and the women's movement, which did weaken stereotypes at some level. In particular, socialization and gender role explanations point to how women and men are taught to accept different roles in politics. Traditional sex role socialization refers to women being taught to be passive individuals who should focus on family responsibilities and building a strong home life, while men are taught to be assertive, independent, and goal-oriented. For Conover and Gray, the distinction is a "division of activities into the public extra-familial jobs done by the male and the private intra-familial ones performed by the female" (1983, 2–3). These distinct roles result in women having fewer political aspirations because they are taught by society to view their roles differently. Politics is viewed as a man's world and inappropriate for women. Surprisingly, although women have clearly broken through educational and professional barriers, traditional sex role socialization continues to weaken women's political ambitions (Fox and Lawless 2003).

For Latinas, political socialization is clearly influenced by traditional gender roles that are similar to those for women in other races or ethnic groups, but they are also affected by cultural traditions that further impede political participation (Hardy-Fanta 1997). In examining the political socialization of Latina women in Boston, Hardy-Fanta contends that Latinas' political participation is "inextricably linked with the development of the political self" and "evolves in conjunction with personal self-development" (1997, 224). As she puts it, there is a process. For some, it is a contemplative and slow process of a growing political consciousness, whereas for others it is "a quick chispa of recognition that a change is needed" (1997, 225).

One source of political socialization for some Latinas is the family. In particular, a politicized family exposes Latinas to politics early in life, establishing political efficacy and making the world of politics more accessible. Although having the support of family when running for office can be one of the most important factors in political development, in some cases the family is not a source of support, but part of the oppression. In response to this oppression, some Latinas become politicized. In other cases, the traditional roles of Latinas as caretakers and mothers may be the stimulus for their politicization. Some Latinas also draw from closely related family traditions and cultural beliefs about "helping others" as a major part of their politicization process (Pardo 1990). As Baca Zinn (1980) points out, moving into politics allows Chicanas and Latinas to alter their traditional sex roles while at the same time retaining and promoting their Chicano culture and identity.[1]

Latinas may also become politicized through a "counter-socialization" experience. Hardy-Fanta (1997) found that some Latinas in her study experienced a counter-socialization as adults: a reorientation or transformation that often runs counter to the expectations of women held by society or the dominant culture. The process of politicization for some Latinas may have taken place during the civil rights movement or the Chicano movement. Gutiérrez and Deen (2000) note that the Chicano movement of the 1960s and 1970s provided Chicanas the experience of and exposure to the power structure. In particular, La Raza Unida, MAYO (Mexican American Youth Organization), and numerous other organizations provided Chicanas opportunities to develop their leadership skills.

Chicana feminists have pointed out how, beginning in the 1960s and 1970s, Chicanas "began to investigate the forces shaping their own experiences as women of color" (García and García 1997, 418). As both women and Mexican Americans, these women wrestled with sexist attitudes and behavior within the larger Mexican American community while also fighting for equality and an end to racism within the larger society. At the same time, Mexican American feminists often did not identify with the women's movement because they were concerned with cultural survival and their families, and because white feminists would rarely address their needs or concerns as minority women. Even the use of the term *Chicana* connoted a feminist ideology that stressed "the interrelationship of race, class, and gender in explaining the conditions of Chicanas in American society" (ibid., 428). Nevertheless, although most Latinas may not identify themselves as feminists, they demonstrate and manifest feminist goals. Most would agree that Latinas also demonstrate a gender consciousness (Hardy-Fanta 1997; Pesquera and Segura 1993).

The literature demonstrates that women who have been elected or appointed to office can emerge from any number of paths of socialization. Politics and political activism may have been consistently present in some of their families, but others may have been politicized by other means or later in life. While political socialization may vary, we do expect a cultural consciousness to be consistently present and emerge alongside politicization.

WOMEN AS CANDIDATES: FACTORS AFFECTING ACCESS TO PUBLIC OFFICE

The Latinas in our study were the first in their respective posts, whether elected or appointed. Consequently, we were interested in learning how they reached their decision to seek political office and, for those who were elected, what their experiences were as candidates. Although Latinas have made great inroads in public office, there are still relatively few, particularly in the higher positions.

Most studies on women in electoral politics consistently find the dominance of women at the state and local levels (Kirkpatrick 1974; Flammang 1984; Darcy et al. 1994). Factors contributing to this general pattern include the level of qualifications, the desirability of the office, level of prestige, proximity of the office, level of commitment, and women's own interest in effecting change at the local level. The eligibility requirements are also less stringent for local and state offices than for federal offices (Darcy et al. 1994). In addition, until recently, local and state governments were considered the traditional arena for women's political participation because the functions and activities of local government centered on caring for the community (Darcy et al. 1994). Despite the preponderance of women in local and state offices, women—and especially Latinas—are far from having proportional representation at these levels.

Generally speaking, we know a potential candidate's decision to run, regardless of gender or ethnicity, is influenced by term limit requirements for the potential office, the presence of an incumbent or the type of seat (i.e., an open seat), and the partisan composition of the district (Duerst-Lahti 1998; Jacobson 1987; Kazee 1994; Stone and Maisel 2003). For most potential candidates, an evaluation of the "opportunity structure" is part of deciding whether or not to run. Along with these factors, some structural arrangements, such as elective or appointive methods, as well as single-member district elections versus at-large district elections, do have a differential impact for men and women, as well as for racial and ethnic minorities. The appointive method and multi-member districts, for instance, are clearly advantageous for women and minorities (Darcy et al. 1994).

Some studies have found few if any differences between male and female candidates. For instance, La Cour Dabelko and Herrnson (1997), in their study of 1992 candidates for the House of Representatives, found few differences in men's and women's campaign styles. Candidates gave similar reasons for running, assembled similar campaign resources, and employed similar strategies and communication techniques. The authors also note that the competitiveness of the congressional race, and not gender, largely dictated the professionalization of campaign organizations. Related to this professionalization are findings that women are able to competitively finance their campaigns, equaling and in some cases exceeding their male counterparts (Darcy et al. 1994; Gaddie and Bullock 1995; La Cour Dabelko and Herrnson 1997; Burrell 2003). Some researchers, however, found that the effect of campaign expenditures varies by gender (Green 2003). Also, it appears voter hostility toward female candidates has declined (Thomas and Wilcox 1998). In sum, these findings may explain why there appear to be no differences between the success rates of male and female candidates, including those successfully competing for an open seat (National Women's Political Caucus 1994; Gaddie and Bullock 1995).

While much of the literature suggests that women and men have similar experiences as candidates, a substantial literature also documents the relevance of gender in various aspects of campaigns. Some studies of political ambition and gender suggest that women use a different calculus in deciding whether or not to run for public office (Burt-Way and Kelly 1992). Specifically, women differ from men in their beliefs about success and their perceptions of the constraints in running for office. Burt-Way and Kelly found that for every measure of success, women are more likely than men to agree that "hard work, ability, and reliance on an extensive system of political, professional, and social connections" helped them overcome any barriers they perceived to their success (1992, 23). Bledsoe and Herring (1990) found that women will seek office when electoral prospects are encouraging and the probability of winning is greatest. Equally important, some research finds gender differences with regard to candidates' perceptions about their qualifications, viability, and electability. Because many women have backgrounds and credentials different from those of men, they are less likely to view themselves as viable candidates and less likely to run for office (Darcy et al. 1994).

In addition to these attitudinal barriers, fewer women are found in the pool from which candidates emerge (Conway et al. 1997; Darcy et al. 1994; Thomas 1998). The eligibility pool argument suggests that candidates tend to emerge from certain professions, such as law and business, and that the scarcity of women in those professions is related to the insufficient number of women as candidates and, therefore, as elected officials. The assumption is that as the number of women increases in these fields, so too will their numbers in elected office. However, as Thomas and Wilcox (1998) show, women are less likely to come from traditional avenues of political office, and more likely to have entered politics from community volunteerism or women's groups. Therefore, a greater representation of women in professions that traditionally feed into political office will not translate into more women in elective office. The eligibility pool of Latinas for public office decreases at higher levels. Some Latinas may have been socialized not to pursue certain "male" occupations, particularly law.

Drawing from a sample of male and female professionals, the group from which most candidates emerge (essentially, the "eligible pool"), Fox, Lawless, and Feeley found that "women in [their] sample demonstrated an interest in seeking office equal to that of men" (2001, 427). Differences between men and women were evident, however, in other areas, particularly in terms of the factors that lead men and women to consider running for public office. Age, income, and the solicitation to run were important to both men and women. However, women were more likely to seriously consider a run for office if they were aligned with the Democratic Party, a member of an interest group, had run for office as a student, or if they held a law degree (Fox et al. 2001). Another difference was that women were less likely than men to consider themselves strong candidates, demonstrating further that attitudinal barriers exist even among women who seemingly have overcome a number of barriers to achieve professional success (Fox and Lawless 2003). While women were as likely as men to assert an inter-

est in running for an elective office, the investigators also found preliminary evidence suggesting that the decision structure affecting women's
decisions to run was more complicated than the one used by men. In effect, the decision-making process of women is more deliberative because
they must consider more factors than men do. This clearly demonstrates
that "merely increasing the number of women in what is considered the
candidate 'eligibility pool' is not, in and of itself, going to alter dramati-
cally the numbers of . . . women elected to office" (Fox et al. 2001, 428).

Also relevant are women's paths to office holding. As alluded to earlier,
women, and especially Latinas, do not necessarily follow the same paths
as men in seeking office. The informal requirements for elective office are
related to education and employment; some Latinas may not have had access to these, or may have been prohibited from attaining them by deliberate and systematic discrimination. Takash-Cruz found that more than
61 percent of public officeholders in California "include community activism in their descriptions of their political experiences," and more than
68 percent had participated in political campaign activity prior to their
first elected or appointed position (1997, 419). Sierra's (1997) examination of
the success story of Santa Fe mayor Debbie Jaramillo as a grassroots activist drew similar conclusions. Fraga et al. (2001) found similar results when
examining Latina state legislators across various southwestern states.
They found that most of these legislators did not have prior elected experience before becoming state legislators and senators, and that most had
gained political experience from their grassroots activism.

Another factor that may explain the limited role of women in politics is
the support or lack of support by party elites. Since women are less likely
to be self-starters or to view themselves as qualified candidates, there is
a greater need for the recruitment of female candidates (Moncrief et al
2001). The most likely recruiters are political parties. Research, however,
is mixed on whether gender discrimination by party elites has diminished
(Thomas and Wilcox 1998; Niven 1998). Although the political parties are
the most visible recruiters, women may be encouraged to run by any number of people, including coworkers, family, and friends. Yet, among the
professionals in the Fox and Lawless study (2003), men are more likely to
be encouraged to run for office by all of the above.

Findings are also mixed with regard to whether women's familial responsibilities limit their participation in politics, sometimes referred to as
role conflicts. On one hand, studies show that male and female candidates
differ in their familial responsibilities, with women having greater private
commitments. When a conflict exists between their political ambitions

and families, women often will choose in favor of their families, whereas men will, more likely than not, choose their ambitions. For instance, Sapiro and Farah (1980) suggest that a woman's role(s) in the family and at work influence the development of, or lack of, political ambition. In particular, the presence of young children in the household is more likely to inhibit or delay women's pursuit of their political aspirations (Bledsoe and Herring 1990; Sapiro 1983). On the other hand, one study shows that among professional women, the presence of children living at home had no effect on whether they considered running for public office (Fox et al. 2001).

Generally, these studies suggest that "when women decide to present themselves to the public as candidates for local, state, and national offices, their chances of winning are as good (and sometimes better) than those of men" (Thomas and Wilcox 1998, 4). Despite overcoming many of these barriers, however, parity in politics has proven elusive for women (Thomas and Wilcox 1998). The question that remains is whether or not these factors affect Latinas as minority women in the same way they affect other women.

When it comes to culture and ethnicity, studies have shown that when one of the candidates is a racial or ethnic minority, particularly if no similar candidate has run before, it galvanizes support, enthusiasm, and turnout among minority voters (Guerra 1991). However, when two or more candidates are racial or ethnic minorities, the issue of race and ethnicity may not necessarily play a central role (Jackson and Preston 1991).

For Latinas, cultural and ethnic elements pervade their motivation to be in politics. In their study of Latina party activists, candidates, and officeholders, García and Márquez (2001) found that Latinas were motivated by a combination of traditionally relevant political concerns and specific community-oriented issues. That is, participants exhibited a commitment to getting particular candidates elected and certain policies addressed, as well as a commitment to both their own communities and the Chicano/Latino community at large. Participants bridged both traditional and community motivations for their political involvement. The authors conclude that Latinas are entering traditional mainstream politics and bringing their strategies from their communities. Moreover, participants voiced a concern to "see others like themselves involved in politics." These dimensions present Latinas as unique in mainstream politics. The research also points to a more robust understanding of the reasons why people become involved in politics.

Culture and ethnicity are also relevant in campaigns for Latinas. In her study of Boston politics, Hardy-Fanta (1993) refers to *"personalísmo"* as having significance for Latinos in electoral politics. In effect, Latino electoral politics involves "face-to-face, personal contact rather than impersonal, quick messages." Moreover, she found that Latina women make references to personal contacts during mobilization efforts more often than men. As she notes, this ties in with feminist literature that addresses the "relational" point of view for women, where women link the individual, family, friendship networks, and community relationships.

García (1998) made similar observations when examining a Democratic primary race for an open seat for the 20th Congressional District, a Hispanic majority-minority district in San Antonio, Texas. Although race did not play a significant role (the three leading candidates were Mexican American), gender, context, and political resources were pivotal in shaping the organization, message, and style of the campaigns. The author concludes that the most formidable challenge for Latinas may be running against other Latinos in highly competitive elections. One way to overcome this barrier is for Latinas to draw on both traditional and grassroots strategies in their campaigns (García and Berberena 2004).

As do other women, Latinas also face barriers when seeking political office or holding office. Latina public officials in California reported that they faced barriers based on race, class, and gender (Takash-Cruz 1993). Some commented that their competency was questioned because they were Latinas. Others commented that they were often "pigeonholed" as representing only the needs and concerns of Latinos, or that their activism within local Chicano organizations was used against them to attack their views (Takash-Cruz 1993). Stereotypes also impact Latinas. As former National Women's Political Caucus (NWPC) president Irene Natividad points out, "minority women must establish themselves as 'credible candidates'; they must be able to raise money and encourage candidates" (Witt et al. 1995, 119). Similarly, Anita Perez Ferguson—a California congressional candidate and the first Latina to run for Congress, as well as a former president of the NWPC—felt that her gender and ethnicity affected her candidacy for Congress in 1990 because minority women have yet to establish their credibility, and the general perception is "not one of competency and leadership" (ibid., 118). As Gutiérrez and Deen note, some Chicana candidates had their husbands campaign for them "to assure male voters that the women would be capable of treating men fairly, especially in cases of domestic abuse and child support" (2000, 7).

Constituting another important cultural challenge for Latina candidates are their family responsibilities. As for most women considering running for elective office, the decision-making process for Latinas hinges on their roles as mothers and caretakers. It is not uncommon for Latinas "to express feelings of guilt, of neglecting their parental and familial duties, even when their children are grown but remain at home" (Takash-Cruz 1997, 426). Many of the Latina public officials in California had children under eighteen, so child care was a major concern, and in many cases, these women had to coordinate the arrangements (Takash-Cruz 1993). Equally important, cultural traditions expect women to fully support their spouses and family. In a study of Texas Chicana county judges, Gutiérrez and Deen (2000) found that age, family size and obligations, cultural bias, marital status, and economic disadvantage serve as barriers for women seeking public office. In addition, the authors found that the lack of political resources, especially when facing incumbents, played a factor in the experiences of Chicanas seeking election as county judge. A symposium sponsored by the Eagleton Institute of Politics in 2003 on Latinas in elections highlighted similar issues. The panelists concluded that the formidable challenges facing Latinas are lack of money, lack of campaign experience and skills, lack of a pipeline, and lack of sponsorship/role models.

García and Márquez also investigated barriers to Latina participation in electoral politics; when asked to consider what were the top three risks for Latinas and Chicanas running for office, participants overall selected "financial burdens, invasion of family and personal life, and the risk of compromising values" as the most important (2001, 118). These Latinas, however, were able to overcome many of the challenges with an enormous amount of confidence. García and Márquez (2001) found that Latinas were extremely confident in pursuing the resources to run for public office. There were, however, variations in confidence levels across age cohorts. The first age group, those born before 1944, were identified as being the most confident because they were willing to serve as a resource for others seeking office. The second age group, those born after 1944 and up to 1962 (the so-called baby boomers), were confident about "seeking information and training others as well as being the first and only Latina running for public office in their community" (García and Márquez 2001, 119). The youngest group, those born after 1962, were most confident, "seeking encouragement as well as identifying people who could impact their political careers" (ibid.). For at least some Latinas, then, their experiences as longtime community activists not only provide an avenue for pursuing political activism or public office, but also a means for overcoming barriers of race, class, gender, and culture in their pursuit of political goals (Takash-Cruz 1993; Sierra 1997).

With regard to running for public office, the literature suggests that many factors affect women's decisions. On one hand, the literature shows that there are gender differences, but on the other, that men and women are the same in many respects. Although women appear to have overcome most of these obstacles, we suspect that the literature has overlooked the experiences of Latina candidates, among whom cultural influences, especially, are still present.

LATINA LEADERSHIP

Within the growing literature on leadership there are different interpretations of what is a leader. In this study, we view public officials as one type of leader, and we were interested to learn about the leadership styles of the Latinas in our study.

Some observers suggest that women and men have similar leadership styles as public officials, but other studies suggest that differences do emerge. For instance, in her study of state legislators, Rosenthal (1998) found that women are more likely to practice "integrative" leadership, while men are more likely to practice "aggregative or distributive" leadership. For Rosenthal, integrative leadership involves "sharing power and empowering others, being noncompetitive and inclusive, seeking consensus and mutuality in relationships, and inviting participation rather than imposing dominance" (1998, 5). Aggregative or distributive leadership is hierarchical, competitive, and involves bargaining and quid pro quo agreements. Among state legislators, Thomas (1994) had similar findings, including that women pursue cooperative strategies and styles, whereas men operate under more competitive tactics.

Research confirms that Latinas have distinctly different perspectives and attitudes (Pardo 1990; Takash-Cruz 1993; García and Márquez 2001). Latinas view politics differently and behave differently as political actors in comparison to Latino men (as noted in García and Márquez 2001). Hardy-Fanta (1993) was among the first to explore gender differences in electoral politics. The male leaders defined politics in conventional terms of political representation and elections, whereas women leaders defined politics as making connections. Latinas also have "a vision of politics that is more participatory" (Hardy-Fanta 1993). Politics entails connections involving people, connections between private troubles and public issues, and connections that lead to political awareness and political action; Latinas, unlike Latinos, reflect a more participatory vision of politics that incorporates cultural needs and expectations (Hardy-Fanta 1993). Latinas also are more likely to manifest their political participation and leadership largely in relation to themselves, their families, and their particular ethnic communities. This important component of Latina leadership is shaped by their unique experiences and political history as minority women (García and Márquez 2001).

In addition, recent literature suggests that Latinas may provide a different style of leadership in terms of the intersectionality of multiple identities (Fraga et al. 2005). Preliminary findings of a recent survey of Latino/a state legislators suggests that Latinas demonstrate an increased capacity to bridge the barriers between women of different ethnic and racial groups, as well as between men and women of different racial and ethnic groups (Fraga et al. 2005).

In sum, most studies suggest that leadership styles reflect gender differences. Like the leadership of other women, Latinas' leadership is characterized by building consensus, inviting participation, and empowering others. Yet, for Latinas, certain cultural elements are present, such as the connection to family and community. They also demonstrate leadership traits that reflect their struggles as minority women, and an awareness of both gender and culture.

LATINAS AS ADVOCATES AND REPRESENTATIVES

A representative democracy necessitates a link between our elected officials and the people they represent. In the structure and function of our political bodies we trust interests to be represented. Political observers argue that in order for substantive representation to take place, people from varying backgrounds and experiences must be included in the policymaking process. Diversity contributes to the advocacy and representation of interests. Representation may come in the form of substantive policy advocacy and constituent representation, or in the form of descriptive or symbolic representation by having people of various racial and ethnic or gender groups elected. As Mansbridge states, "Descriptive representation enhances the substantive representation of interest by improving the quality of deliberation" (1999, 628).

One central question underlying this research is whether the "perspectives and behaviors of women differ significantly from those of men" (La Cour Dabelko and Herrnson 1997). Female candidates are more likely than their male counterparts to advocate for social or "compassion issues," such as children's issues, poverty, education, and health care. Focusing on the U.S. Senate, Kahn (1993) found that female candidates are uniquely advantaged in certain campaign environments where social issues are salient, and women are viewed as more competent in these areas. These studies suggest that in some areas women convey a perspective that is unique to women, which may at times be to their advantage.

Numerous studies on women and politics focus on the impact that women have once in office. Women legislators are more likely to give higher priority than men to issues that relate to women's rights, education, health care, families and children, and the environment (Hawkesworth 2003). Women are more likely to support feminist positions on women's issues and actively promote legislation to improve women's status in society (Carroll 2004). Studies show that women and members of racial and ethnic minority groups, as elective representatives, have policy preferences distinct from those of their colleagues (Vega and Firestone 1995; Poole and Zeigler 1985; Thomas and Welch 1991; Clark 1998; Swers and Larson 2005; Bedolla et al. 2005). Vega (1997) explored the behavior of female and ethnic minority legislators in the Texas legislature and found that both women and minority legislators are more likely to introduce and enact gender- and ethnic-related bills. Moreover, the introduction of gender-related bills is less affected by such factors as group cohesion or group seniority than by an increased percentage of women in the entire legislature.

Equally important, a study of congressional women revealed that women perceive their representational roles as "surrogate representatives" (Carroll 2004). In other words, most women in Congress felt a common bond and identity with women outside of their districts, and the necessity to represent women's interests. These views, and representational responsibility to women, are significant in demonstrating how the institutions themselves are changed with the presence of women (Carroll 2004).

Do Latinas make a difference once in office? Takash Cruz found that Latina public officials in California "will challenge existing gender relationships as well as racial inequality between nonwhite and white women" (1997, 429). In addressing whether Latina representatives practice "a politics of difference," the author contested that while Latinas support feminist agendas, they "express more concern with issues facing the Latino community as a whole, such as employment, access to education and retention, and safe neighborhoods, issues largely stemming from institutionalized racism and classism" (ibid.). Latina public officials also face challenges similar to those of all women. Gutiérrez and Deen (2000), for instance, in their study of Chicana county judges in Texas, found that these women faced hostility from an establishment that viewed them as political outsiders.

From a theoretical perspective, Fraga and Navarro (2004) suggest that the increased Latina success in attaining formal elective office must be linked explicitly with insights provided by writings and scholarship on Latina feminism. The authors contend that the literature on Latino and Latina politics can be divided into two analytical categories: descriptive differences and prescriptive possibilities. The first category is more traditional, identifying descriptive differences between Latino men and Latinas, that is, public opinion, political participation with special emphasis on grassroots leadership, and electoral representation. The second category, prescriptive possibilities, focuses on Latina feminist writings that present models of Latina legislative leadership. Unlike the first category noted above, this literature develops a theoretical understanding of the transformative (i.e., institution-changing) potential for innovative ways of conceptualizing the interests of Latino communities and creating strategies for policy advocacy built on the intersectionality of Latinas in the American polity.

Research on gendered institutions finds that women face significant challenges in building on their increasing presence when attempting to make institutions more responsive to the legitimate interests of groups who have been historically underrepresented, including women (Steinberg 1992; Kathlene 1994; Kenney 1996; Rosenthal 2000). However, research also finds that many female elected officials do tend to bring distinct perspectives and leadership styles to legislative arenas (Kathlene 1989; Acker 1990; Thomas 1994; Tamerius 1995; Sparks 1997; Rosenthal 2000; Carroll 2001; Walsh 2002; Jeydel and Taylor 2003). It may be that Latina intersectionality will force Latina legislators to face even greater barriers to their success within the masculinized and racialized institutions that all legislatures tend to be (Crenshaw 1989, 1997). Research suggests that this is also the case for African American women who are legislators (Darling 1998; Barrett 2001; Smooth 2001; Hawkesworth 2003). However, it is also possible that the intersectionality of Latina representatives provides them with a greater selection of strategic options to pursue the building of coalitions of interest and legislator support. It ultimately allows them to use their multidimensionality (Segura 1986; Anzaldúa 1987) to credibly advocate on behalf of a multiplicity of interests simultaneously.

Given the literature on representation, Latinas, like most women, will demonstrate a propensity to advocate for women and families. But, different than most women, Latinas will also advocate for issues affecting the Latino community. Their experiences as minority women—the intersectionality of gender and ethnicity—will be reflected in their advocacy and in their strong cultural identity.

POLITICAL CULTURE, GENDER, AND ETHNICITY: THE TEXAS CONTEXT

Since this book centers on Latinas in Texas politics, a brief review of the role of political culture, gender, and ethnicity is in order. Elazar's (1984) theory of political culture addresses the influence of a state or region's beliefs, values, and experiences on a state's politics or policies. Elazar constructs a typology of three political subcultures: moralistic, individualistic, and traditionalistic.[2] Elazar identifies Texas as a combination of the traditionalistic and individualistic. Generally speaking, Texas politics has been shaped by the hierarchical relations of the Old South, based on race, gender, and class. It is also influenced by the rugged individualistic mentality of the wild frontier, where government does not play a central role, and where skepticism and cynicism towards politics and politicians exist. Elections are characterized by lower voter turnout, and participation is largely discouraged (Brown et al. 2003).

These embedded values and beliefs have relevance for women and minorities in public office. Research has indicated that women are more likely to run for office in states that support women in politics, such as states where a moralistic political subculture dominates. In contrast, in states where traditionalistic and individualistic subcultures dominate, such as Texas, women are less likely to run for office and get elected, particularly to state legislatures (Thomas and Wilcox 1998). This political subculture suggests that politics has been and, to some extent, continues to be dominated by an established male elite, a "good ol' boy network," and longstanding conservative views regarding the role of women. Clearly there are vestiges of this political culture influencing women's political behavior. As most studies find, there are simply not enough women running for legislative office (Darcy et al. 1994; Carroll 1994).

Political culture also impacts the role of racial minorities, particularly Mexican Americans in Texas, with regard to politics. There is clear evidence, for instance, of the extensive restrictions on the voting rights of racial minorities (Davidson 1990; DeLeon 1993). Furthermore, this interpretation of the impact of political culture on the politics of Texas only accounts for the values of the dominant social and ethnic groups. As Hero points out, "the political values and beliefs of racial minorities and non-European groups were not considered in the political culture framework" (1998, 9). Hero contends that racial/ethnic diversity is an important component of a state's politics and policies. The author identifies states by their degree of diversity: homogeneous, heterogeneous, or bifurcated. State politics and policies are products of the cooperation, competition, and conflict between and among dominant and subordinate minority groups. As minority diversity increases, a state moves from a moralistic political subculture to an individualistic subculture, and eventually towards a traditionalistic subculture. Hero contends that in states such as Texas where traditionalistic and individualistic subcultures dominate, a heterogeneous and, especially, a bifurcated society exists. This has implications for the view of minorities in elective office. Although Hero does not directly address the issue of representation of Latinos in elective office, it is expected that a state's diversity has an impact. Specifically, in a bifurcated society, there is an orientation to a social order that is hierarchical, based on class, race, and gender. Arguably, Latinos have reached some level of success in elective office. However, it should be noted that this success has taken place regionally, primarily in south Texas, where Latinos dominate. Equally important, Latinos have been elected primarily in local and state legislative elections, with fewer, if any, winning statewide or federal offices.

While political culture is relevant in Texas politics, so is the role of gender. Few studies have examined the role of women in Texas politics (Boles 1984; Stanley-Coleman 1996; Potter 1998; García 1997; Jones and Winegarten 2000). Boles (1984) contends that despite the fact that Texas has produced a number of prominent female politicians who have acquired a reputation for unusual political effectiveness, the reality is that women's political participation in Texas falls below the national average. Boles points out that Texas women have acquired an "archetypal" portrayal of Texas women in politics. Drawing from the rugged, individualistic tradition of the western frontier woman, a mythology has surrounded Texas women such as Barbara Jordan and Ann Richards (and, more recently, U.S. senator Kay Bailey Hutchison and Texas comptroller Carole Keeton Strayhorn). The 1990 gubernatorial race between Ann Richards and challenger Clayton Williams symbolized how gender affected voters' behavior (Tolleson-Rinehart and Stanley 1994). Richards epitomized the challenges women often face as candidates in that she had to convince voters that she could lead, yet she was feminine enough to ease their fears about women in powerful positions.

Stanley-Coleman's (1996) research on Texas women candidates found that in 1994 a record number of women sought office, particularly at the statewide level. She notes that a total of twenty-one women ran for statewide or congressional office, yet their rate of success (43 percent) trailed that of men (54 percent). Equally important, Republican women made the greatest gains, reflecting the national and statewide trend towards Republicanism. This trend was further solidified in 1994 with the election of Republican George W. Bush and the defeat of Governor Ann Richards. One should note that the 1994 gubernatorial election was one of the closest in Texas history. Republican women running for office were clearly elected on the coattails of George W. Bush. This trend continues to the present in statewide, judicial, and legislative elections.

Another relevant study of Texas women focuses on the leadership positions held by women serving in the state legislature. Potter (1998) examined the number of women serving as legislative leaders and committee chairs, and on what are referred to as "Mega" committees (those considered the most politically powerful). Although some women have served on the six Mega committees, a female legislator had never served as chair in either house, nor have women served as legislative leaders, indicating that women have not gained access to powerful positions in the Texas state legislature. Since the study, some women, primarily Anglo and Republican women (with a few exceptions, such as Senator Leticia Van de Putte) have served on these committees. García (2001), in her examination of Texas women legislators in the 1990s, found that beginning in 1994, Republican women continued to close the gap with Democratic women in both the house and senate. By 2001, female Democrats and Republicans were roughly equal in both houses. Republican women are also making strides at a faster pace than Democratic women. These trends have important implications when considering alliances forged along gender, party, and/or ideological lines.

UPCOMING CHAPTERS

The preceding literature review provides the reader with an overview of the research that relates to our four areas of inquiry and other relevant issues. Expectations with regard to these areas of inquiry have also been raised. In the next six chapters, the authors investigate the levels of office that Latinas in Texas have achieved.

CHAPTER 3

IRMA RANGEL

The First Latina in the Texas Legislature

I didn't know I was going to be the first one. I felt like I was really going to have to deliver. If I didn't succeed, they were going to say, "All Mexican American women are failures."   TEXAS REPRESENTATIVE IRMA RANGEL

INTRODUCTION

In 2006 there were nine Latinas in the Texas legislature: seven in the house and two in the senate. These women must credit Irma Rangel for blazing the trail for Latina leadership in state politics. Elected to the Texas House of Representatives in 1976, Rangel was the first Hispanic woman to serve in the state legislature,[1] the first and only Latina to chair the Mexican American Legislative Caucus (MALC), and the first Hispanic—male or female—to chair the House Committee on Higher Education, a major standing committee. She also was the first female district attorney in Corpus Christi and the first woman to serve as chair of the Kleberg County Democrats. In her own words, Rangel entered politics to "give voice to the voiceless." With this purpose, she was a tireless advocate for public policies that benefited the lives of poor women, children, and racial and ethnic minorities until her death on March 18, 2003.

Rangel's altruistic commitment to public service is perhaps best illustrated by the fact that she served more than twenty-six years in the Texas House of Representatives and never ran for any other public office. This required her to campaign for reelection every two years for a position that pays an annual salary of only $7,200. Because of the low salary and short term, the rate of voluntary turnover is typically high among the

150 members serving in the house. The average turnover rate is 20 percent (Kraemer et al. 2001).

Unlike most state legislatures that convene annually for seven to nine months, the Texas legislature meets in regular session every two years for only 140 days. Although the governor occasionally calls the legislature into special session, and there is some out-of-session committee work, legislators usually have full-time occupations and view their legislative responsibilities as part-time. In sharp contrast, Rangel closed her law practice in 1993, and for ten years her only job was serving as state representative for District 43.

To better understand Representative Rangel's political ambition and policy motivation, this chapter begins by reviewing what is known about her early socialization, education, and work experience prior to her decision to run for office. The middle section focuses on that turning point in her professional life and the experience of her first campaign and the barriers she faced. The final sections examine Rangel's leadership style and policy advocacy.

POLITICAL SOCIALIZATION

Rangel's interest in politics, her work ethic, and her seemingly overriding motivation to help those struggling for a better life are largely due to her parents' life experiences and their involvement in city politics while Rangel was growing up (Rangel 2000). From her parents, Rangel learned the importance of hard work, independent thinking, and the necessity of vigilance in the struggle for a better life, "not just for ourselves, but for all people." She described her parents as "hustlers," but also as "hard-working, self-made persons" who "truly wanted to help other people" (Rangel 1996, 4).

Rangel was born in Kingsville, Texas, in 1931 to Presiliano M. (usually called "P.M.") Rangel and Hermina (Big Minnie) Lerma Rangel. Her father, orphaned at the age of five and with no formal education, was a migrant worker until he trained to become a barber. He eventually became one of Kingsville's most successful business leaders, owning two barber shops, a bar, and several stores.

Rangel's mother dropped out of school after the fifth grade when her father, her only living parent, died. Married before she was twenty, Minnie soon bore three children. However, P.M. and Minnie did not have a typical marriage for that time period, with the wife staying at home and depending on her husband. Encouraged by her husband to be independent, Minnie went into business for herself as a traveling salesperson, or peddler, on the weekends, selling dresses and other items from the trunk of her car to poor women in surrounding areas who lacked the transportation to shop in town. Rangel and her sisters would take turns going with their mother to sell candy to the children of her mother's clients. Over the years, Minnie's business prospered, allowing her to open a permanent, full-time dress shop. Rangel worked after school at her mother's store or at one of her father's businesses until she left for college. She recalled both her parents providing assistance to less fortunate acquaintances, "want[ing] to share with others what they had not been able to achieve for themselves" (Rangel 1996, 5). Her father also was very active in the local Democratic Party and the Good Government League, an organization that sought to expand and improve the quality of government services through the implementation of fair elections and municipal reforms. The league sponsored ballot initiatives and endorsed candidates, and P.M. was responsible for organizing many of the group's rallies and meetings. He also attended the Democratic Party's state convention. According to Rangel, the townspeople knew that her father was very active in his efforts to improve the community, and they looked to him when deciding whom to support in elections because "they trusted that he was going to select the best candidate for the benefit of the community" (ibid.).

Rangel's older sister, Herminia (or Little Minnie), also was independent-minded and involved in local politics. A pharmacist and the first local Mexican American woman to open her own drugstore, Little Minnie also was the first woman elected to the school board and later became the school board president. The local prominence of her parents and sister were an asset when Rangel began running for political office.

Rangel lived at home until 1952, when she graduated from Texas A&I University with a degree in business administration and teacher certification. After college she taught for fourteen years—initially in Texas, then California, and finally in Caracas, Venezuela. Besides teaching business courses, Rangel served as a bilingual teacher, a math teacher, and a principal. She also wrote textbooks on how to teach Spanish in elementary grades. However, she wanted to be doing more for the Hispanic community (Rangel 2000).

At a time when few Latinas had even a single college degree, Rangel decided that additional credentials would increase her ability to help others. In 1966, at the age of thirty-five, Rangel entered law school at St. Mary's University in San Antonio. After completing her juris doctorate in 1969, she worked as a law clerk for U.S. District Court Judge Adrian Spears in San Antonio. In 1971 she moved to Corpus Christi, where she served as assistant district attorney for a year and a half before she briefly joined a private practice. In late 1973, she returned to Kingsville, where Rangel and her partner, Hector García, were the first Mexican Americans to open a law office. For many years Rangel was the only Latina attorney in Kingsville (Rangel 1996, 7).

At the urging of former professors at Texas A&I, in 1974 Rangel began her involvement in partisan politics when she agreed to run for chair of the Kleberg County Democratic Party. Interestingly, Rangel denied having the political ambition to think of the local party office as a stepping stone to running for higher office (Rangel 2000).

THE DECISION TO RUN AND THE FIRST CAMPAIGN

In the fall of 1975, Rangel attended a two-day conference in Austin co-sponsored by the Lyndon Baines Johnson Presidential Library and LBJ School of Public Affairs. Coordinated by Liz Carpenter, former press secretary for President Johnson, the conference focused on the topic of "Women in Public Life." It was Rangel's experience at this meeting and the specific encouragement of other Latinas in attendance (including Dr. Cleotilde García, Marta Cotera, Paulina Martinez, Lupe Tovar, Olga Solis, and Lupe Angiano) that convinced her to seriously consider running for the state legislature (Rangel 1996, 10).

More than a thousand people attended the conference. Some of the diverse topics discussed at the meeting included common problems for women around the world, media coverage of the women's movement, and the gains and gaps for women in the power structure of Texas. The long list of speakers and panelists included leaders in the women's movement, government, politics, and journalism. There were four plenary panel discussions in addition to fifteen workshops, and nearly fifty women participated as speakers, panel discussants, or workshop leaders. However, only two Hispanic women, Dr. Cleotilde García and Marta Cotera, had speaking roles, and both were asked to limit their remarks to two minutes.[2]

Cotera began her remarks by telling the audience that she had been given only two minutes to speak, but since she had a lot more to say, she would ignore the time limit. After lamenting the lack of Mexican American women on the conference organizing committee, in national political organizations, and at various levels in the federal government, Cotera's comments focused on the absence of Chicanas at the state level: "in Texas, we have no state senators, no state representatives, no judges, no mayors, and only one Chicana on a state commission."[3] A later speaker who also addressed the status of women in Texas concluded that the conference's success would be directly measured by whether women attending the conference felt less intimidated expressing their views; whether they would go home and organize, petition, and attend meetings of their local governments to ensure more social service funding for women's needs; and whether the number of women running for and being elected to office in Texas increased significantly.[4]

Rangel felt very empowered by the speakers' messages, although she was surprised by how few Mexican American women attended the conference and really bothered by their lack of representation among the conference leaders. "Because [whenever] you looked up at the stage, we could see only Anglo-American women and one or two Black women but no Mexican American women except for Dr. García who had been up there for a minute or two, and then Marta [Cotera], but that was it. So we felt like we had to do something about the absence of Mexican American women involved in this politics" (Rangel 1996, 10). At some point during the meeting, the Latinas went outside to discuss the issue, and according to Rangel, eventually they all pressured her to do something to remedy the situation.

Because the incumbent house representative in Rangel's district, Greg Montoya, was under federal investigation, he was considered vulnerable. The Latinas at the conference, who were also members of the Women's Texas Political Caucus (WTPC), felt the time was right for someone to run against Montoya, and they specifically encouraged Rangel to do so. Spearheaded by Paulina Martinez, a prominent WTPC member from Dallas, caucus members continued to encourage Rangel to run against Montoya in the weeks following the meeting. Finally, after talking it over with her parents, she decided to "take a crack at it" (ibid., 10–11).

Rangel was the last candidate to enter the race for state representative. In the Democratic primary, she faced Montoya, the incumbent, as well as another Mexican American man from the town of Elsa and an Anglo-American woman from Rivera. In the seventies, Texas was still a strong one-party state, so it is not surprising that there were no Republicans seeking the office.

Rangel had several things going against her when she ran the first time. First, she had been back in the Kingsville area for only a short period after being away for more than seventeen years. Many people did not know her or remembered her only as a little girl. Rangel credited her parents' and sister's popularity and good reputations for helping her overcome this obstacle—first when she sought the chair of the Kleberg County Democratic Party, but, more important, when she ran for state representative a year later. "They had always been loved and respected so I remember going to a Bingo and saying . . . I am Irma Rangel, you know, P.M.'s daughter *y la hermana de* [and the sister of] Minnie. . . . [The people reacted with] oh, well, this is good and then they started applauding" (ibid., 11). Rangel frequently took her parents with her on the campaign trail, even having them sit with her when she attended a televised candidate forum. Her sister went door-to-door with her in Kingsville and also rode with her in a car caravan that traveled the entire district.

Other obstacles for Rangel included her gender and marital status. Being a female lawyer and candidate for state representative was a novelty at that time. Rangel believed that some men were initially very skeptical and reluctant to support a female lawyer for political office. Also, Rangel was not married, and there was gossip, even among her supporters, that she might be a lesbian. In actuality, she had once been engaged, but her fiancé had been killed in an airplane accident while serving in the military. Rangel told the story of how one of her major supporters, the mayor of Elsa, called her to say he was very concerned, very worried, and that she had a big problem that he needed to discuss with her, but not over the phone. Rangel agreed to drive to Elsa and meet him in the back of the grocery store he owned. When Rangel arrived, the mayor was there with several other men who surrounded her and accused her of being a lesbian. Rangel denied being a lesbian and said she was sorry: "And I am looking at them, you know, and telling them that I am very sorry . . . [but] I am not going to go to bed [with you] to prove it to you because I wasn't desperate to get elected" (ibid., 22).

Although her gender and marital status may have initially limited her support among men, Rangel had great support from women, especially those in the rural areas of her district. With the help of her family and the strong support of Latina farm workers, Rangel ran a successful grassroots campaign during the primary and managed to make the runoff, facing Jean Hines from Rivera. Hines was from a well-known political family, her father having been the Kleberg County commissioner for many years. State representative Gonzalo Barrientos went down from Austin to help Rangel campaign, and she held her first political rally. For the first time, she also used campaign donations to purchase radio time and candidate cards and brochures. Her largest donation, $1,850, was from the Texas Women's Political Caucus. Rangel remembered spending only $9,800 on her campaign, the bulk of it on gasoline, radio ads, and candidate cards (ibid., 25). She relied heavily on the word-of-mouth efforts of volunteers and in-kind donations such as overnight lodging in the homes of friends, office space for campaign headquarters, and lots of homegrown and homemade food for Rangel and her volunteers.

Rangel won the runoff election by almost a two-to-one margin and, with no opponent in the general election, was off to Austin as a state representative and the first Latina to serve in the Texas legislature. Rangel told the *Corpus Christi Caller-Times,* "I didn't know I was going to be the first one. I felt like I was really going to have to deliver. If I didn't succeed, they were going to say, 'All Mexican American women are failures'" (Danini 2003).

Rangel did not fail, and her success in the legislature inspired other Latinas to run for state office. Moreover, Rangel must have more than satisfied her constituents because she never lost a reelection bid. In fact, in fourteen consecutive campaigns, she was seriously challenged only once. In 1988, after redistricting added several new counties to her district, including Starr County, Rangel faced a strong challenge from former Starr district attorney Pancho Cerda. This forced her to hold her first official fund-raiser to raise needed funds for radio and television ads to counter the negative media messages of her opponent. After a dirty campaign in which Cerda accused her of being a Communist, frequenting exotic bars, and a host of other things, Rangel won the election by less than two hundred votes. Although Cerda demanded a recount, it did not alter the outcome of the election (Rangel 1996, 39).

LEADERSHIP STYLE

Initially, Rangel had little in common with most of her legislative colleagues, but she was outgoing by nature and not easily intimidated. To be an effective legislator, Rangel had to develop mutually respectful and cooperative relationships with representatives sharing similar policy goals, many of whom were Latino. It took some time for her to build those relationships, but Rangel recalled that the Latino members treated her nicely, although "sometimes too nicely" (ibid., 29). Believing they were being overprotective, she told them:

> "I know how to hold my own guys, so don't worry." And so when they found out how I could talk to them, you know, *pero yo les decía así como me decían ellos porque soy mujer, ultimamente se más que ustedes.* [I would say to them like they said to me because I was a woman, ultimately I know more than you.] [Eventually] I was one of them. But not to go drink beer. . . . I didn't look for that. (ibid., 29–30)

In the early years of her tenure Rangel avoided informal gatherings with Latino legislators. Both her gender and single marital status probably made it difficult for her to comfortably socialize with most of them. As Rangel explained, "they did not ask me to go drink beers with them . . . [but] I didn't hang out with the lobbyists either . . . just went up there and did my business" (ibid., 30).

As the only Latina representative from 1977 to 1985, Rangel felt the burden of being "first" and worried about appearing less qualified or less prepared than her male colleagues.[5] Not wanting to be patronized by lobbyists or legislators, she worked very hard to be taken seriously. Perhaps subconsciously motivated by her mother's belief that Latinas must work and study twice as hard as everyone else, Rangel worked long hours and strived for perfection in all of her work. She generally expected everyone else to do the same and could be very intimidating in her demeanor, acquiring a reputation among both staff and colleagues for "being tough" (Leo 2003).

Rangel's reputation among constituents provides an interesting contrast. Leo Zuniga, as director of governmental and public relations for the Alamo Community College District (ACCD), testified before Rangel's House Committee on Higher Education on many occasions. He characterized Rangel's persona in the obituary he wrote for her in the ACCD quarterly newsletter:

> Whenever witnesses representing higher education appeared before her committee, she would always soften the attempts of harsh grilling from other committee members. Her smile was friendly and reassuring. Her smile would boost the confidence of those appearing before her committee. She radiated energy and warmth. (Zuniga 2003)

Over the next several years in the legislature, Rangel was able to develop close relationships with many of her Latino colleagues. One longtime colleague, legislator Paul Moreno, characterized her as "our den mother" who advised and encouraged younger lawmakers: "She never tired of telling me, 'Vote your conscience, you won't go wrong.' I know she did" (quoted in Danini 2003). Rangel initially earned their confidence and trust with her strong professionalism and considerable knowledge of the legislative process. For these reasons, she was asked several times to run for chair of the Mexican American Legislative Caucus, but she declined, primarily due to other commitments associated with her law practice in Kingsville. In 1993, however, she finally consented to run and, with little opposition, was elected as the caucus's first Latina chair. At that time she closed her law office and devoted 100 percent of her time to her responsibilities in Austin (Rangel 1996, 36).

The short Texas legislative sessions make passing legislation a challenge for even veteran members, but first-time legislators are especially disadvantaged. Typically, they do not know the maze of formal rules and standard operating procedures that enable the legislature to complete its work, and some legislators never completely learn the system. Rangel, however, quickly mastered the process. To accomplish this feat, she said, "I listened a lot. I observed a lot and I read a lot" (ibid., 34). She also was smart in her first hiring decision, choosing Angie Flores as her first administrative assistant. Having previously worked as the legislative aide for Governor Preston Smith, Flores was very familiar with the people and the process.

Throughout her tenure in the legislature, Rangel selected Latinas as her administrative assistants, usually recent college graduates or those in the process of completing their college degrees. As previously noted, Rangel held everyone to very high standards, but she also took great interest in her assistants' lives, nurturing them and encouraging them to set high goals. Myra Leo, her assistant from 1980 to 1984, recalls Rangel always saying, "Prepare yourself better than anyone else. . . . Hard work pays off. . . . I want you to leave here with the skills to be able to work anywhere and be successful. . . . I have great confidence in you and in your abilities. . . . You can do great things if you focus on helping others" (Leo 2005). Leo also recalls that Rangel trained and led staff members by her own example, assisting in daily office duties such as greeting visitors, answering phones, and personally following up on constituent requests. Rangel would say, "I am no big [bleep], we are all the same" (ibid.).

It took several terms for Rangel to have much impact on policy decisions, at least in terms of successfully authoring major legislation. She was not hesitant, however, to express her opinion—sometimes on very controversial issues—during committee or floor deliberations. In her first floor speech Rangel spoke in favor of an amendment to a bill penalizing women for seeking abortions that would exempt women who were victims of rape or incest pregnancy. She said she was moved to speak about the issue because of the tragic circumstances she had encountered while serving as an assistant district attorney, when she had to tell victims of rape and incest that they could not get abortions or they would risk being sentenced up to ten years in the state penitentiary.

Rangel remembered asking and receiving permission from Sarah Weddington, who was fighting the entire bill, to speak in favor of the amendment.[6] In her floor speech, Rangel did not hold back in telling about the experiences and emotions she dealt with as a prosecutor, and she also said, "I do not condemn nor do I condone abortion but . . . it was not right that we, and [especially] you men here, to be telling a woman whether or not she has the right to her privacy, to her own body. And so this [amendment] has to go on" (Rangel 1996, 32).

Today the issues of rape and incest are more openly discussed, and allowing abortions for women who are involuntarily impregnated is fairly widely supported, but in 1977, when Rangel and others spoke in favor of the amendment, there was complete silence on the floor following their remarks. Rangel's pointed words to the male members also positioned her on the side of feminists and pro-choice advocates, groups that were not popular with most house members.

Rangel's concern for women, especially those without money or power, was further evident in the first bill she successfully introduced. The bill was to establish a state program to provide job-related education and training to women on welfare. The program was the idea of Lupe Anguiano, a civil rights activist and former nun who ran a similar program for Mexican American female heads of households living in public housing projects in San Antonio. Working with Anguiano, Rangel recalled easily persuading legislators to authorize the program:

I said, "All right, guys, you want us to have babies, then help us support them. . . . Let us help those who cannot help themselves and make them self-supporting and all that. This is a wonderful program," and I think that is all I said and poof, the bill passed. (ibid., 33)

Problems arose, however, because the appropriations bill needed to be amended in order for the program to be funded. Rangel described the events when the appropriations bill came on the floor:

. . . all the speaker's lieutenants were going up and down. They didn't want the appropriations bill to change or anything. So then my amendment came on to get monies for the program. And there was a lot of smoke and a lot of noise going on and everything and I say, "Shoot, I am going to start shouting." I want them all to hear me. . . . So I start hollering and all this noise [is still] going on and I am practically shouting in the mike and then all of a sudden, Bang! What was that? A light bulb de allá arriba [way up there came down]. All the glass came on down. . . . Smith Gilley was the one that got all the glass on his head and everybody was very quiet. Everybody got scared . . . so I got on the front mike and I said, "All right members, someone up there is trying to tell you something. I respectfully request [that] you vote for my amendment," and it passed. (ibid.)

Rangel seldom minced words in her personal conversation or public remarks. She also was inclined to use colorful or salty language, primarily for emphasis, according to staff and longtime associates (Fikac 2003). With her loud, cackling laugh and a habit of calling everyone, even fellow legislators, "baby," Rangel may have given casual observers the impression that she was a Hispanic Phyllis Diller, a popular Anglo comedian during the early 1970s. But she could not have been more serious about her legislative service (Leo 2005).

Rangel was a person of strong convictions and was known to stand up to the most powerful leaders in state government to defend the issues she cared about. For example, her bill to establish a law school in south Texas passed in the house but died in the senate when Lt. Governor Bill Hobby criticized the proposal, saying that it was ludicrous to spend scarce money on a law school in south Texas. In a message, Rangel responded, "How can you say that? You have got three law schools in Houston and that is not ludicrous" (Rangel 1996, 48).

In an interview with José Angel Gutiérrez, Rangel (1996) admitted that she was not generally considered a "team player" by the legislative leadership, who were Democrats during all but the last two years of her tenure; this is perhaps one reason why she served thirteen years before she was given a committee chairmanship. Perhaps Rangel was not a team player, but she knew how to play the legislative game, and she played to win. One particular case, the passage of the Top Ten Percent Plan, exemplifies her political savvy and leadership skills.

Simply explained, the plan guarantees admission to Texas public universities and colleges for all Texas high school students who graduate in the top 10 percent of their class. The plan was formulated in response to the 1996 decision of the U.S. Court of Appeals in the case of *Hopwood v. Texas*, which invalidated the affirmative action component of the admission process at the University of Texas–Austin School of Law. The *Hopwood* decision effectively ended affirmative action practices in public universities and colleges throughout the state. The result was a significant decrease in the already low percentage of African American and Latino/a students admitted to the state's flagship universities: the University of Texas–Austin and Texas A&M (Holley and Spencer 1999).

Rangel and other like-minded leaders hoped to eventually overturn the *Hopwood* decision, but they also wanted to devise a constitutionally sound model for university admissions that would ensure both diversity and the inclusion of highly qualified students. Although not directly involved in the plan's initial formulation, Rangel helped to organize, and closely co-operated with, the task group that authored the bill, and she then took the lead in persuading legislators of the proposal's merits (Leo 2005).[7] For many Texans, the plan's key selling point was its de-emphasis on using standardized testing to largely determine college admission. Instead, students who demonstrated an extended pattern of high academic achievement and hard work as measured by their cumulative grade point average would be rewarded with college acceptance (Hair 2001).

For Rangel, supporting the policy was a "no brainer" because it would result in as many, if not more, poor and minority students being admitted to the best universities in Texas as before the *Hopwood* decision due to the high degree of segregation in Texas public schools. She knew it would result in a more diverse and better-educated workforce, which would strengthen the state economy and ultimately benefit all Texans. Finally, she hoped that it would strengthen the relationships between public high schools and colleges as administrators became more aware of and interested in the quality of their newly admitted students (Rangel 2000).

Early in the legislative process, Rangel and the task group members met with Terrell Smith, the attorney who had represented Cheryl Hopwood in the lawsuit against the UT School of Law and who was subsequently appointed as Governor George W. Bush's legislative counsel. In a 1997 interview, Rangel's rationale for meeting with Smith, a conservative and an opponent of affirmative action, was pragmatic and to the point: "I heard a rumor that the Governor has the veto" (Hair 2001, 29). Apparently Rangel and the other task group members were successful in persuading Smith of the plan's merits: days later, they were informed that the governor would not veto it. Although the governor stopped short of an endorsement, Rangel felt it was a positive sign that she could press forward in moving the plan through the legislature (ibid.).

In her capacity as chair of the House Committee on Higher Education, Rangel scheduled multiple hearings on the issue of diversity and declining minority enrollment at flagship schools, thus giving task group members and other supporters numerous opportunities to publicly testify on behalf of the Ten Percent Plan. By offering her cooperation on his legislative priorities, Rangel also brought into her legislative coalition one of the legislature's most conservative and powerful members, Republican Senator Teel

Bivins, who was also chair of the Senate Higher Education Committee (ibid.). Rangel's cooperation with Bivins throughout the session is illustrative of the saying that Rangel frequently repeated when advising her staff and younger colleagues: "remember it's better to work with honey than vinegar" (Leo 2005).

Sometime during deliberations of the plan, the Speaker of the House, Pete Laney, requested a meeting with Rangel. Task group members suspected that Laney was going to ask her to delay action on the bill, possibly for several years. Praising Rangel's "strategic skills," Gerald Torres, who also attended the meeting, characterized it as "pure political theater" (Hair 2001, 28). Rangel brought with her nine Mexican American experts, including political scientists, sociologists, demographers, lawyers, and historians. As reported by Torres:

> When the Speaker and his colleagues said "we need to study this," Representative Rangel stood up, waved her arm expansively, slowly pointing to the assembled group of the state's leading Mexican-American academics. Then, turning to the Speaker, she said decisively, "We've studied it." The Speaker dropped the idea of a study and . . . we never had to say a word. (ibid., 29)

Ultimately, House Bill 588 establishing the Ten Percent Plan was narrowly passed by a nonrecorded vote, with most members voting along party lines, although, notably, the Republicans on Rangel's committee supported the bill (Holley and Spencer 1999). With the endorsement of Republican Bivins, the bill passed in the senate with a wide margin of support. Three days later, Governor Bush signed the bill into law.

A broad range of political observers credit Rangel's leadership and determination for the successful outcome (Holley and Spencer 1999; Fikac 2003; Leo 2005; Hair 2001). Rangel took the lead in moving the Ten Percent Plan legislation through the house while simultaneously working to ensure the cooperation and support of party leaders, including Republican governor George W. Bush. To accomplish this legislative victory, Rangel helped build a strong bipartisan, multiracial coalition. She also effectively neutralized the potential opposition of both Republican and Democratic leaders.

REPRESENTATIONAL ROLE AND POLICY ADVOCACY

Rangel clearly was aware of her ethnicity and minority status as well as the significance of her presence in the legislature. During her early years in office, tourists and other curious people would come up to her and say: "I just want see what the first Hispanic woman looks like" (Leo 2005). Her participation and leadership in Hispanic organizations—not just in MALC, but also in the Mexican American Democrats, the Mexican American Bar Association of Texas, and the Hispanic National Bar Association—demonstrate her strong commitment to the substantive representation of Hispanic interests.

Rangel's primary identification with Hispanics, more specifically Mexican Americans, overshadowed her identification with women or even Latinas. Although she supported many of the same policy goals, she was not active in women's organizations. Rangel expressed delight regarding the increasing number of Mexicanas in the legislature and actively supported them in their bids for leadership, but she did not see the need for Latinas to organize separately. Instead, she was more concerned with maintaining the unity and success of the Mexican American Legislative Caucus; however, had the opportunity arisen, Rangel would have supported the leadership of a Hispanic male over that of an Anglo woman (ibid.).

As a first-term representative Rangel immediately focused her advocacy efforts on policies and programs to address the limited educational opportunities and other problems common to her poor, rural, and minority constituents. She sponsored legislation covering a wide variety of issues during her tenure, including making the registration process of the Texas Department of Transportation easier and less expensive for vehicles transporting seasonal agricultural products, extending the absentee voting system, funding the first state-built roads in Starr County, and creating shelters for victims of domestic violence. Nevertheless, Rangel retained her initial policy emphasis on education and social welfare throughout her twenty-six years in the legislature. The boundaries of her district would change considerably during that time period—to include more counties, more urban areas, and considerably more people—but the basic demographic profile of the district she represented, and the people she cared about most, remained essentially the same.[8]

Rangel's main policy focus and the bulk of her legislative contributions were in the area of education, particularly higher education. Throughout her career she labored to bring high-quality, accessible education to Texas students in both secondary and higher education. She directly impacted community college systems throughout the state by providing the necessary leadership for successful passage of legislation that exempted certificate and vocational occupational students from the Texas Academic Skills Performance exam (TASP) (required for students to graduate from high school), provided dual credit enrollment opportunities to high school students, and authorized community colleges to offer remedial education to high school students. As previously detailed, in 1997 Rangel secured the passage of landmark legislation, the Ten Percent Plan. During the same session, she successfully sponsored a bill that provided tuition and fee exemptions to instructional aides pursuing teaching certificates.

The limited state funding for higher education and the lack of professional and graduate schools in southern border towns and the Rio Grande valley was a major concern for Rangel because of their direct impact on her constituents. In 1993 Rangel was instrumental in passing legislation that brought border colleges and universities more than $450 million in additional funding. The South Texas Educational Initiative Fund provided the start-up money for the valley's first community college, South Texas Southern. Although Rangel's efforts to establish a law school in the valley were ultimately unsuccessful, in 2001 she authored and helped to pass the law that established and funded a new school of pharmacy at Texas A&M–Kingsville. Subsequently renamed in her honor in 2003, the Irma Rangel School of Pharmacy is the first professional school in south Texas. Besides her legislative efforts to support higher education, Rangel generously and regularly contributed her own money for scholarships and other events to benefit students in the Rio Grande Valley (Leo 2003).

Rangel's advocacy efforts also were directed at assisting low-income families. As previously described, she introduced and helped to pass legislation assisting low-income mothers with dependent children in 1977, and in 1981 she successfully sponsored the Good Faith Donor Act, which exempted stores and manufacturers from liability for donating food to the needy.

Rangel also worked to increase access to health care for poor people, many of whom were located in rural areas. In 1997 she was the primary sponsor of legislation creating the Texas Health Service Corps Program (THSCP), which provides stipends to primary care physicians who make the commitment to practice in federally designated medically underserved areas in Texas. She also supported the establishment and expansion of the Children's Health Insurance Program and the County Indigent Health Care Program.

Over the years, Rangel consistently voted to establish and/or increase funding for education, health, and human services programs, and consistently voted against proposals that would cut programs, limit eligibility, or reduce benefits in these areas. In her mind, it was the government's responsibility to assist the working poor, students, and children, and she was very passionate in this belief (Rangel 2000).

CONCLUDING THOUGHTS ON IRMA RANGEL

Smart, independent, and self-assured, Irma Rangel had the courage to challenge and change the status quo. She left a successful career as an educator at the age of thirty-five to train for a new career in law, and after receiving her degree, she broke gender barriers with every subsequent career move. Unquestionably, Representative Irma Rangel was a trailblazer. Her adult life was a series of Latina "firsts." However, her contributions go well beyond symbolic representation.

Rangel made a significant difference in the lives of the people she served, and in the actions and decisions of fellow legislators. She believed in the power of education, hard work, and social justice. She also believed in doing more to serve the Hispanic community. Her policy priorities and legislative accomplishments reflected those beliefs, which were also evidenced in the way she conducted her life and in her interactions with others. Rangel's record of policy priorities serving low-income minority families and her twenty-six-year tenure as a member of the Texas House of Representatives, during which she never sought higher office, proves that her political ambition was defined by her commitment to public service.

Rangel was an exceptional leader who knew how to connect with people and persuade them to do the right thing. She frequently led by example, giving her time, talent, and personal wealth unselfishly to help others. Her leadership was widely recognized even by those who disagreed with her political beliefs. It is important to note the respect and support she received from Republican leaders. In 2002, when Republicans became the majority party in the house, Rangel lost her position as chair of the House Higher Education Committee. However, the new Speaker of the House, Tom Craddick, asked Rangel to remain in the leadership as vice chair of the committee, the only Democratic leader from previous years who was asked to continue in a leadership position.

Rangel was a fighter, not only on the floor of the legislature but also in her personal struggles. She was seventy-one when she finally succumbed to cancer after having fought the disease for several years—first in the form of inflammatory breast cancer, then ovarian cancer, and finally brain cancer. Throughout her treatments she continued to work, wearing colorful hats to cover her balding head. She remained a constant forceful presence in the legislature right up until the last few weeks before her death.

At her funeral, her priest at Our Lady of Guadalupe Catholic Church in Austin, Father J. C. Cain, characterized Rangel's life work as "a vocation dedicated to helping the poor and marginalized, bettering the Hispanic community, and fighting for justice and equality" (Fikac 2003). On a lighter note, in remarks that caused many in the audience to laugh and nod their heads in agreement, Father Cain commented on Rangel's passion for doing right and her compassion for people, saying, "I think she would have been a wonderful priest. . . . She would have made it to being the pope. . . . She could have been the first female pope—the first female Hispanic pope" (ibid.). More seriously, Irma Rangel was not only a unique individual, but also a remarkable Latina leader.

CHAPTER 4

LATINAS IN THE TEXAS SENATE

I think the expectations are higher because there haven't been that many [Latinas in the Texas Senate] and you are represent[ing] not just females, but an ethnic group that has not always been afforded the opportunity to participate in the political process.   STATE SENATOR LETICIA VAN DE PUTTE

. . . there are not enough women who have figured out how to balance [faith and family], how to prioritize, but I believe that the younger women will make a difference . . . that as they grow up professionally and politically, that you will see more women in the ranks.   STATE SENATOR JUDITH ZAFFIRINI

INTRODUCTION

In the history of the Texas Senate, only two Latinas have served as senators, and this chapter examines their political biographies. It is important to note that compared to other state senates, the Texas Senate is relatively small given the size of the state and its 254 counties, and despite its increasing population over the past decades. The senate is composed of only thirty-one members, each elected from geographically distinct districts drawn by the members of the Texas House of Representatives and Senate. As a result of the 2000 Census, each senator represents approximately 673,000 people.

Texas senators serve four-year terms, with no term limits. Aside from citizenship and age requirements (the minimum age is twenty-six), the only other requirement is that senators must reside at least one year in their districts preceding a general election. Although there are no educational requirements, most senators have law or other professional degrees.

The senate was designed by the framers of the Texas Constitution in 1876 as an amateur legislature, meaning senators are paid only a token salary (currently $7,200 a year), but they also receive a per diem allowance and a generous retirement package. It is also important to note that until 1997, the Texas Senate and its leadership had been controlled by Democrats, albeit primarily conservative ones. In 2007 the senate had twenty Republicans and eleven Democrats.

Long dominated by Anglo men, only twelve women (including two Latinas and two African Americans), fifteen Latinos, and seven African American men have served in the history of the Texas Senate, according to the Legislative Reference Library.[1] During the 80th Legislature in 2007, there were only four women, six Latinos, and two African Americans in the senate. In addition, only Anglo men have served as lieutenant governor, the presiding officer of the Texas Senate. The lieutenant governor is elected statewide, and the position is considered one of most powerful in Texas politics.

Both Latinas elected to the Texas Senate are Democrats. Representing predominantly Hispanic districts, Judith Zaffirini was first elected to the senate in 1986, and Leticia Van de Putte was elected more than ten years later. Senator Zaffirini, a native of Laredo, represents Texas Senate District 21, a large and diverse district that stretches across several counties, including Webb (Laredo) and parts of Bexar (San Antonio). Unlike most Latina public officials, Senator Zaffirini holds a postgraduate degree: a Ph.D. in Communications from the University of Texas–Austin. She married Carlos Zaffirini soon after high school and has one son, Carlos Jr., who graduated from the University of Texas School of Law and the McCombs School of Business. In addition to her responsibilities as a state senator, Zaffirini runs her own business, Zaffirini Communications.

Senator Van de Putte represents District 26, centered in San Antonio. In a special election in 1999, after serving in the Texas House of Representatives for five terms, she became the second Latina elected to the Texas Senate. Van de Putte also attended the University of Texas–Austin, where she earned a pharmacy degree. A pharmacist for more than twenty years, she too is a business owner. The senator and her husband of almost thirty years, Pete, have six children. Senator Van de Putte was elected by her Democratic colleagues as chair of the Democratic Caucus after the close of the 2003 regular session. In her position as chair, Van de Putte quickly gained national notoriety when she led her Democratic senate colleagues to Albuquerque in order to break quorum during a special legislative session in the summer of 2003. In an unprecedented move, the Republican-controlled legislature attempted to redraw Texas's congressional districts with the goal of ultimately increasing Republican membership in the U.S. Congress. Although congressional redistricting eventually took place, it was only after the Democratic senators drew considerable national attention to the issue.

Since there have been only two Mexican American women senators in Texas politics, examining these women's backgrounds and ascendance to public office may bring us a step closer to answering why there are so few. This chapter focuses on four factors: 1) political socialization, 2) their decisions to run for public office and the barriers that they faced, 3) Latina leadership, and 4) representational roles and advocacy.

POLITICAL SOCIALIZATION

What is perhaps most notable about both Latinas in the Texas Senate is their early exposure to politics. Zaffirini was influenced by the political involvement of her parents and her parents' friends, as well as by her paternal grandfather, who was originally from Greece and later served on the Laredo City Council. She remembers handing out fliers, phoning potential voters, and participating in "pep parades," beginning when she was only five years old. In her words, "I don't remember *not* being involved in politics—we just grew up that way." Her family was very active in the Democratic Party, and she recalls campaigning for presidential candidate John F. Kennedy when she was in high school.

In addition, in earning an advanced degree Zaffirini was able to further refine her skills as a political candidate and public official. For instance, she credits her critical thinking skills for allowing her to carefully evaluate policy issues before debating them on the senate floor, and her Ph.D. training also gave her the skills to develop survey instruments used by her pollsters. She recalls that when asked by her campaign consultant how she was able to remain so calm during her first appearance before the editorial board at the San Antonio Express-News, she said it was "a piece of cake" compared to sitting for her oral exams.

Senator Van de Putte was also introduced to politics early in life. Her godfather is Joe Bernal, a prominent figure in San Antonio politics. First elected to the Texas House and later to the Texas Senate, her godfather was elected statewide to the Board of Education in 1996. She remembers as a young child wearing a "Vote for Bernal" T-shirt. As she points out, her parents and family became actively involved in local politics when their "compadre" ran for office. She continued to be active in politics before running for office herself, campaigning for a number of different candidates, planning fund-raisers, and helping with mailings. She was also active within the Democratic Party, serving as precinct chair in the 1980s.

THE DECISION TO RUN FOR THE TEXAS SENATE

The literature cited in Chapter 2 suggests the decision to run for public office can be very difficult, especially for women. Unlike most public officials, state senators must be willing to travel (in some cases long distances) to Austin on a regular basis. As mentioned in Chapter 3, they are expected to be present during the regular session, which is roughly 140 days from January through May in odd-numbered years unless a special session is called by the governor. Consequently, senators must be able to make sacrifices in their full-time jobs, both professionally and financially. State senators are also very visible and powerful policymakers in Texas politics. For that reason, senatorial races are often very costly and competitive, requiring extensive fund-raising.

A number of factors influenced both senators' decisions to run for office. One notable characteristic is that both of them faced a slate of mostly male candidates in competitive open races. Also notable is that particular issues motivated both women to run for office. Having the support of their families, particularly supportive spouses, and a core group of friends was equally important in their final decisions to run for office—and in their eventual success.

For Zaffirini, the push to run for public office evolved from a series of discussions: "my friends and family members and I decided that I had the greatest opportunity to run and win, and meet the goals that we identified as important." One reason she wanted to run for state senator is that she felt "we needed a state senator who would be in touch with the people of the district, and who would tackle not only the most challenging issues, but also the local issues that were important to people in the city or in the county, and that was the kind of senator I wanted to be." Zaffirini had been working since the 1960s to establish a four-year university in Laredo, and she considers higher education not just a priority, but a "passion." After she decided to challenge the current incumbent, it appeared that she might actually win, and he withdrew from the race, attracting a slate of three male candidates in the primary. She forced a runoff election against William (Billy) Hall Jr., winning sixteen of the twenty counties, and then won the general election, facing Republican Bennie Bock, by less than five thousand votes. Since being elected to the senate, she has not faced any serious challengers. Part of the reason she continues to run for the office is her unwillingness to be a "lame duck," and her belief that it would be virtually impossible for a Laredoan to be elected if she retired, given the multi-county district she represents.

Van de Putte's family and spouse were also pivotal in her initial decision to run for public office. She and her husband had regular discussions regarding public health issues, and as a pharmacist and business owner, Van de Putte became increasingly concerned with health policy. For example, she couldn't understand why the state would pay hundreds of thousands of dollars for a hospital stay for a premature baby,

> but they wouldn't spend the $1.11 a month for prenatal vitamins and prenatal care. . . . It didn't make sense to me that our state had a comprehensive policy that said every cow in this state must be vaccinated, must have full immunizations; but we had no such policy for children, and that was because cows were economic development; but children were not perceived as [a part of our] economic development.

In addition to the state legislature's lack of emphasis on health care, Van de Putte identified a need to draw attention to children's issues, as well as those affecting small businesses.

The first opportunity to run for a state house seat presented itself in 1990 when the incumbent for District 115, Orlando García, resigned his seat to run for the Fourth Court of Appeals. Van de Putte's husband is the one who suggested that she run for office, and who had the greatest influence on her decision. She admits that neither of them believed she could actually win the race since she had no political experience and had six small children at home. However, she was convinced she should enter the race when she overheard her son explain to her youngest daughter that their mom needed to run because "there were not enough mommies in the state house." As she explains, "It just clicked . . . there's not enough mommies making the decisions; and I think that when you exclude the talent pool particularly in policymaking and you don't have different backgrounds, different careers and [both] genders, then all you have are male-dominated decisions." For Van de Putte, the realization that different perspectives were needed in the state legislature provided further impetus to run for public office.

Van de Putte also had to consider the viability of the other candidates. Two prominent Democrats were already vying for the nomination when she initially considered running. Nevertheless, her husband convinced her that even if she lost, she could at least draw attention to specific issues. As it turned out, Van de Putte forced a runoff for the party nomination and ultimately won the general election with more than 71 percent of the vote. She concedes that although she never had "a burning desire" to hold office, she has loved it ever since first being elected.

After five terms in the Texas House, Van de Putte decided to run in a 1999 special election for an open seat representing the 26th senatorial district, vacated by the late Senator Gregory Luna. She was among five candidates (three of whom were men) in a highly competitive race, but she ultimately won the special election with 45.7 percent of the vote. In the 2000 Democratic primary, when she was challenged by a man, she won 54.4 percent of the vote, and then won the general election unchallenged.[2] During her second term, she was recruited by her peers (eleven Democratic senators) to chair the Democratic Caucus—a significant position given that by the 2003 legislative session both the house and senate were controlled by Republicans, and there were no Democratic officials statewide. A decision to accept the position would, in effect, make her the leader of the Democratic Party in Texas. After much persuasion by her colleagues, she accepted the position after the end of the regular session. As described earlier, the ensuing battle in the Texas legislature over redistricting propelled her into the national arena.

BREAKING BARRIERS TO PUBLIC OFFICE

The literature cited in Chapter 2 suggests that women are overcoming many of the barriers they once faced, but whether all women, regardless of race or ethnicity, face similar barriers or are overcoming existing barriers at similar rates remains a lingering question. Although both Van de Putte and Zaffirini were successful in their bids for the Texas Senate, they faced various barriers, including those related to being Latina. In addition to their familial obligations, both faced difficulties in fund-raising and campaigning. They also cited cultural factors that may be particular to Latinas, as well as structural factors affecting any potential candidate for the Texas Senate.

Family responsibilities continue to be a challenge for women running for office, especially for Latinas. For both Zaffirini and Van de Putte, the major obstacle to running for public office was their familial obligations. According to Zaffirini, she had to consider her ability to prioritize her commitment to "faith and family" first and foremost. Her decision-making process involved figuring out how to balance her personal priorities and holding public office. This dedication to faith and family made her decide to *not* run for the state senate in 1982, when her pregnancy, after seventeen years of marriage, took precedence. Later, heavy campaign schedules and the position itself demanded longer hours, so she would often be at work as early as 4 A.M. so she could return early in the evening, or leave for work later in the day and stay at the office in the evening to make time for her family. Whenever possible, she tried to avoid spending evenings away from home. As she points out, "My son did not spend one night without either of us until our twenty-fifth wedding anniversary . . . [when] he was eight years old." Zaffirini decided early in her career to not campaign on Sundays until right before the election. Instead, she reserves Sundays for attending Mass and spending time with her family. Even after eighteen years as a senator and her son grown and no longer living at home, she says there must be a compelling reason for her to accept an invitation to attend functions on Sundays, such as "a family event that my husband and I could attend, or a huge rally the Sunday before the election."

Zaffirini acknowledges that balancing faith, family, and a career is a key hurdle: "I cannot see how I, myself, I'm not saying another woman can't . . . could run for governor or lieutenant governor or Congress and prioritize faith and family and balance my business interests. If I could see that, perhaps I would [run for higher office]. I'd love to run for governor. I would love to have the responsibilities of being the governor of Texas or the lieutenant governor, [but] I don't see how I could. . . ." However, Zaffirini did pursue the office of lieutenant governor when given the opportunity. On December 28, 2000, the Texas Senate convened as a Committee of the Whole for the first time in Texas history to select one of their own as lieutenant governor to replace Rick Perry, who became governor when George W. Bush resigned to become president. Although all of the senators' names appeared on the original ballot, approximately half of them, including Senator Van de Putte, asked to be removed from the list before the first vote. Senator Zaffirini, the last Democrat to be considered, remained in competition until the sixth ballot.[3]

Van de Putte's familial obligations were also a consideration in her initial decision to run for public office, and they continued to play a role in her decisions to seek higher office. When she first considered running for the state legislature, Van de Putte had six small children, all under the age of ten. When she did decide to run for office, many Latinas would ask about her familial responsibilities. She recalled one particular occasion when some Latinas asked, "Who's going to take care of your children?"

And I said, "My husband."
   And they said, "Your husband is going to babysit your kids?"
   And I said, "No. My husband doesn't babysit. My husband does parenting. I don't babysit my kids."

Although surprised by such questions, Van de Putte explains that the only reason she could even consider running was that she had the full support of her husband and children, as well as her extended family. Her commitment to her marriage and children remains her top priority, and she says she would walk away from life in the public sector if her marriage or children were ever in trouble.

Although women appear to be catching up with men in their ability to raise funds, both Zaffirini and Van de Putte believe it is still the greatest challenge for women interested in running for the senate. Van de Putte raised about a million dollars in five months but says, "That's tough to do." Zaffirini's perspective has also been shaped by her experiences with fund-raising. Her first campaign was extremely expensive, and she credits her husband for helping raise the necessary money. For her first race in 1986, she and her husband knew they would need about $300,000 to run a successful campaign, but she recalls, "I didn't know how to raise money at that level." As mentioned earlier, the incumbent withdrew from the race, leaving the door open for five male candidates to vie for the seat. The large field of primary candidates led to a runoff election, which was also costly. Zaffirini ultimately won the general election facing a Republican challenger, but being a contender in all three elections cost almost $700,000, more than double what she and her husband had projected. She was forced to borrow more than $300,000, which she says was not completely repaid until the late 1990s.

Van de Putte also highlighted the difficulty of fund-raising, particularly for Latinas. Although women must be willing to raise money, asking for it can be especially difficult for Latinas since their communities and culture expect them to be humble and hospitable. Van de Putte says her grandmother would always say, "Oh, mi'ja, don't be boastful of yourself." But, she says, being humble just "doesn't cut it when you're running for office." She recognizes these characteristics as a wonderful part of the culture, but often contrary to what is needed to successfully run for office. As she points out, "You have to be so self-assured. You have to ask for money. You have to be willing to ask for votes . . . and yes, you have to have a huge ego to be able to put up with the public scrutiny of a campaign." She also explains how her mother's and grandmother's generations still believe that politics is not dignified for women because it requires "getting down and dirty." But Van de Putte is convinced that "politics is about advocacy" and "it's real life." Besides, she believes that "things are beginning to change in the last decade and a half."

The grueling campaign itself can also be a barrier for candidates. Although Zaffirini believed her early exposure to politics and her life experiences had prepared her for her bid for the state senate, she admits her first campaign was still an eye-opener. For one, she was surprised to learn that having an advanced degree from the University of Texas–Austin could be portrayed as a potential flaw by her opponents. In particular, because she attended the university during the 1960s, her opponents tried to depict her as a "U.T. hippie," implying she used drugs. Her response was to agree to a drug test on an instant's notice in order to disprove the charges. She was also confronted with the abortion question when her opponent falsely portrayed her as being pro-choice. Although Zaffirini is a Democrat, she is also a practicing Catholic who considers herself pro-life. What she found most surprising, and disheartening, was that people would actually believe she was pro-choice simply because her opponent said so.

Another significant barrier for potential candidates is the institution of the Texas Senate itself. Because the salary is so low, anyone considering a run for a Texas Senate seat must be able to absorb the financial cost, and they must also have a flexible work schedule to allow for legislative sessions—requirements that few can afford. As Van de Putte points out, "I know many great folks who would be wonderful public servants, but their families can't afford it."

Once in office, breaking through established alliances in the state legislature can also be a significant barrier. Women, in particular, often experience difficulties breaking into the "good ol' boy" networks. Zaffirini recalls "old-fashioned" barbeques in her district that were open to men only. For one particular barbeque event, only male attorneys and male judges were invited. That event has since been opened to include female attorneys and judges, but only after some prodding. The common practice of excluding women may still hinder female candidates and public officials.

One way that women have overcome this barrier has been to form their own networks—a survival strategy that has been a key component of Van de Putte's success. She has been an active member of the Mexican American Business and Professional Women's Association since 1980. As she explains, the women in this organization have helped her tremendously in her election efforts, through their financial donations, acting as volunteers, hosting parties on her behalf, and providing support. Working in a male-dominated field, pharmacy, and having just had a baby when she first joined, she could relate to the other women in the group because they, too, had to balance a family and a career. According to Van de Putte, "They understand culture and they understand that family comes first. They understand some days . . . you go to Mass and you go to your mama's house or your grandma's house and they understand. Or my kids are sick and I have to take them to the doctor. But they also understand when grandmothers are sick or . . . in the hospital. They are a great support and great friends." In recognition of this network, Van de Putte displays a pair of red high-heeled pumps and a red purse in her district office. The shoes are a reminder that she is, like the other women in the group, a Latina and a "hoochie mama." And the red purse is a reminder of the importance of pay equity for women, especially Mexican Americans.

Both Zaffirini and Van de Putte believe societal and cultural factors may discourage Latinas from seeking elected office. Specifically, Zaffirini believes we have few Latina leaders "because more women don't run and win. . . . There are not enough women who have figured out how to balance, how to prioritize." She believes that Latinas, in particular, struggle against traditional roles since they overwhelmingly handle the responsibilities at home and are often discouraged from getting involved in the political arena. The challenge may be even greater for Latinas who are professionals, she says, "because many women are still expected to play the traditional role at home and [they] have many responsibilities. . . . They will face many difficulties in meeting these responsibilities." However, she believes that change will occur as younger women, who are not tied to old stereotypes and traditions, make choices about their professions. According to Zaffirini, "Younger women are growing up with more opportunities and, in many cases, the same future that is available to men." This is in contrast to Zaffirini's own experience:

> I didn't grow up with a vision of a great future. I didn't grow up with an idea of being a senator or even being a professional or having a Ph.D. I didn't consider going to college until I was a senior in high school. . . . Now, little girls can grow up thinking about running for office, of being a professional, whatever that profession may be. Being an astronaut, or an architect, a lawyer or doctor, a governor or president. But we didn't have those role models.

Finally, the risks of running for public office are often higher for Latina and Latino candidates, according to Van de Putte.

> The expectations are higher because if you fail at something it's not just a disappointment to your family or friends or the people you represent, it's a disappointment to a people. . . . I'm a female and I'm

Hispanic and so if I do something wrong or if I don't measure up, it's a reflection not just on me personally, but because there haven't been that many Hispanic females, it's a reflection on [other] Hispanic females, and that's a lot of pressure.

Since both Van de Putte and Zaffirini are experienced candidates, they were asked to offer advice to Latinas interested in running for public office, specifically for a senate seat. Zaffirini suggests that women first get their priorities straight: "If family is important to you, regardless of how you define family, make sure it is at the top, and then address the issue of how you can balance your personal priorities with public service and with business." She also points out that women typically do not have experience fund-raising and networking in the political arena. Her own experiences have highlighted the need for women to obtain these kinds of skills. According to Zaffirini,

Many women don't have experience in raising money, and you cannot win without a good campaign treasury. It's very expensive to run for office. And there are many men who have greater expertise in raising money. . . . I always recommend to women who are interested in politics that they get experience raising funds. There are women who have experience in raising funds for civic organizations, but many of those women are not interested in the political arena, so I wish that more of them were because they have that ability.

Van de Putte's advice to Latinas interested in running for office is "know yourself, know yourself." She suggests that if the motivations are power and excitement, then maybe another profession would be better.

Because in order to do a good job as an elected official, doing what's best for the people and from your heart are necessary for serving in a representative democracy. . . . You've got to know in your heart that you are really doing this . . . for the people. You want to do a good job, it's got to be for the people that you represent. If it's about you, you may end up being successful for a while, but you won't end up being a public servant. . . . When women say they are thinking about getting into politics, I would say, "Love your neighborhood, and get involved at the local level in your neighborhood organization, at your churches, at your schools, nonprofits, and see if you like people. Because if you don't, politics is not a place for you."

In addition, Van de Putte warns that women must be able to accept criticism. Campaigns can get ugly, which can hurt not only the individual running for public office, but the entire family.

LATINA LEADERSHIP

Given that Van de Putte and Zaffirini were the first Latina senators and leaders within their communities, both were asked to describe the qualities of a good leader as well as their own leadership styles. Zaffirini believes that "in many cases, leadership requires vision and commitment, inspiration, dedication and communication skills . . . so many skills are necessary." And she prefers "transformational" to "transactional" leadership: "A transactional leader is one who deals in good and bad, reward and punishment [whereas] a transformational leader is one who hopes to develop future leaders. And that's what I believe is a hallmark of a true leader." A good leader, she says, is "someone who is not only interested in leading, but who also knows that to lead, you must sometimes follow, and you must always be a good team member, but that at the same time, your goal has to include developing future leaders."

In reflecting upon her own leadership skills, Zaffirini claims, "In myself, I see the ability to articulate issues and the ability to organize. The ability to be committed and dedicated, and certainly the ability to inspire others to do good and do better work as necessary." When asked how she thought others would describe her leadership, she stated, quite simply, "articulate, organized, and hardworking."

Van de Putte believes "vision, passion, and a sense of humor" are also important characteristics of a good leader. "Maintaining a good sense of humor is important when dealing with the human condition . . . knowing that human nature is such that everything doesn't always progress as planned, and that people can be very hurtful and deceitful, and that's human nature. . . . So, I think a sense of humor . . . keeps a person focused on not taking everything so seriously." In reflecting on her experience, she reveals that she felt unprepared for the job when she was first elected to the legislature. She had assumed that the decision-making process would be a rational one, where policy issues were evaluated for advantages and disadvantages, and then debated and adopted. But she quickly learned that, in actuality, it was a very personal process: "It's about relationships. It's about having trust in the system [and] getting to know your colleagues. And the most important constituency for a state legislator is the other legislators that you have to get to vote on your bill or your public policies."

In her position as chair of the Texas Senate Democratic Caucus, Van de Putte has worked on establishing personal relationships. She attributes her success to "having a good understanding of people—what they want and why they feel they need something." She believes her professional work as a pharmacist has given her experience in building personal relationships. She genuinely cares for her patients, and this characteristic has transferred into her political work as a state senator as well as chair of the Democratic Caucus. Another important leadership quality that she sees in herself is a clear understanding of the state's changing demographics, which she believes makes her a better policymaker: "I know that I am good at getting people to work together for a common goal. I manage a very large family, and I share that with my husband."

The senators also were asked to point out the most important issues affecting women, specifically Latinas. Not surprisingly, both senators agree that educational attainment and opportunity are at the top of the list. Van de Putte believes that Latinas need to be "self-sufficient and independent," which can only be accomplished by getting an education. For Zaffirini, having an education also means "not only being bilingual, but multilingual, and not only bicultural but multicultural." Both also acknowledge the importance of affordable and accessible health care.

REPRESENTATIONAL ROLES AND ADVOCACY

How public officials view their roles as representatives greatly influences their style and advocacy. One important aspect of being a representative, particularly as a minority, is how one identifies oneself. A label signifying ethnic ancestry can vary depending on the situation, geographic region, level of politics (local, state, or national), and immigrant status.

Both senators demonstrate a sophisticated understanding of their ethnic identities. Zaffirini prefers calling herself "Mexican American, part Greek, with burnt orange blood."

> . . . because we live on the border, and here we use the term "Mexican American." We do not use the term "Latino." In fact many people don't like it. They like "Mexican American" because we live on the Texas-Mexico border. So our heritage really is Mexican American, or Texas American . . . and I like that term, without a hyphen. And then "part Greek" because my paternal grandfather came from Greece, and "burnt orange" because I bleed burnt orange. I have three degrees from U.T.–Austin.

Zaffirini's ethnic identity is also connected to the importance of being bilingual and bicultural. She points out how her mother always stressed "the importance of speaking English with an American accent and Spanish with a Mexican accent."

Van de Putte jokes about her own ethnic identity, saying that the labels that best describe her are "probably 'mommy mujer,' probably 'Latina'. . . . I prefer the term 'Latina' to the term 'Hispanic.' I like the word 'Chicana,' but it embodies more of a California-type Latina. And I would really say that I'm a Tejana." As a ninth-generation Mexican on her father's side, Van de Putte is very proud of her Mexican American heritage and culture. As she points out, "I can't disassociate who I am. . . . You can't dissociate what you have been through in your background. . . . I bring to the table things that [come] from my background." Her strong racial consciousness has also been influenced by the discrimination she has encountered. She vividly remembers being sent home from school in the third grade for speaking Spanish, and she was publicly humiliated for her writing skills by one of her professors in a pharmacy class because she was "Mexican." She also remembers being told how her grandmother was hit with water hoses the first time she tried to vote, and how her mother had to pay taxes and take a literacy test before being allowed to vote: "She took the test with three people, and two of the others did not pass. So they said she was in a group that didn't pass [and] she didn't get to vote."

Another area of representation is influenced by gender, and both senators reflect a strong gender consciousness. Zaffirini explains,

> Someone said that women comprise half the population. We should comprise half of the Congress and half of the legislature. . . . You'll see the book I have on the stand there, and you can see that the pages are yellowed. That book has been opened . . . to a page that says . . . "whatever women do, we must do twice as well as men to be thought half as good. Luckily, this is not difficult." I quote her all the time.

She also recognizes that society's expectations are linked to gender and ethnicity. For instance, she points out how the criteria for being a leader is different for Latinas than for other women "as a matter of expectations. . . . But the children of today will grow up with equal expectations for boys and girls when they are men and women. . . . We didn't have those role models." Zaffirini believes that one reason attitudes toward women in the workforce are changing is that "today's CEO, who is typically male and who didn't have a mother and a wife who worked, now has a daughter who won't stay at home . . . and that's the difference." When told by a voter that women belonged at home cleaning house instead of running for office, Zaffirini responded, "Yes, sir, that is exactly what I'm doing. I dusted off in May, I swept up in June, and I'm going to mop up in November" (Jones and Winegarten 2000).

Van de Putte's gender consciousness has also been shaped by her experiences. She vividly remembers being one of only eight women of color in her pharmacy class of sixty-five students. Her subsequent experiences as a pharmacist in a male-dominated profession were also influential. Equally important, she witnessed how difficult it was for her mother to support her family while trying to complete her college education. But Zaffirini, like Van de Putte, also believes that attitudes towards women are beginning to change. She points out that more women, and Latinas in particular, are holding offices and starting their own businesses rather than choosing conventional professions as teachers and nurses. Nevertheless, she also points out that the reason why women are primarily teachers and nurses, and why there are shortages of both, is because these professions are "gender specific and usually lower paid," and also less valued.

As part of their representational roles, both Van de Putte and Zaffirini have the ability to serve as advocates and influence public policy. As the literature suggests, it is not unusual for female legislators to focus on policy areas that relate to women's issues and the family. Both senators focus on policy areas that traditionally relate to women, and their accomplishments are tied to their initial motivations for being in politics. To get a sense of how effective they have been as public officials, we asked them to describe their most significant accomplishments. Zaffirini believes she has had the most impact on health and human services (as chair of the Health and Human Services Committee) and education policy (as a member of the Education Committee). She helped to pass legislation creating a four-year university in Laredo (Texas A&M International University), as well as the Laredo campus of the University of Texas Health Science Center. These particular accomplishments are important to her because these are "higher educational opportunities that will make a difference for the families of this region and persons from outside this region, from other countries who will come here to secure an international education." Other accomplishments include legislation punishing drunk drivers, and other legislation with the goal of immunizing all children in Texas.

Van de Putte also places a strong emphasis on health and human services, and she identified the Children's Health Insurance Program (CHIP) as one of her accomplishments. She is dedicated primarily to policies that affect "the quality of lives of more people and families." She also identified her leadership of the Democrats in the Texas Senate as another accomplishment. In reflecting on breaking quorum during the redistricting dispute, she said holding the senate Democrats together was critical. She also recalled that this particular task was so difficult because it meant leaving their families behind, physically leaving the state, and moving to Albuquerque for at least thirty days while the special session was being held. When asked how she managed to keep the senate Democrats together, the only way she could describe herself was as "a kind of momma," a role she is comfortable with as the mother of a large family who is used to mediating disputes, knowing when to allow individuals to work out their differences and recognizing when to intervene.

CONCLUSION

Senators Van de Putte and Zaffirini are trailblazers in many respects. They both have advanced degrees and are successful professionals. Neither chose politics as a primary career path, although both women were exposed to politics early in life and were politically involved before making the decision to run for office. Second, although both women faced barriers to running for public office, they were able to overcome them. Both had small children when they decided to run for elected office, and both emphasize that family is their top priority. As described elsewhere, having supportive partners and families, including extended families, was essential in their decision to run for and remain in public office. Their success can be attributed, at least in part, to the fact that both women were well established in their professional lives by the time they entered politics. Another factor is that being a Texas senator is not a full-time job, allowing them to keep their priorities straight. A barrier for both women was the significant cost of running a campaign, but again, both were able to overcome the financial constraints, a challenge they acknowledge could discourage other Latinas from seeking office.

Also contributing to their success is the dedication of both senators to policy areas that traditionally relate to women: education and health care. Although the short sessions can make it difficult to be effective in the Texas Senate, the fact that both Latinas play key leadership roles helped them to pass important legislation and influence the policy agenda.

Finally, it bears repeating that Latinas are an anomaly in Texas politics, but these two women became the first elected to the Texas Senate. As the eligibility pool continues to increase, and Latinas continue to run for and win senate seats, they will be in a prime position to be important policymakers.

State representative Irma Rangel speaking before the House Chamber, 1986. 69th Legislature. Courtesy of Texas State Library and Archives Commission.

State senator Judith Zaffirini in 2006. Photo courtesy of Senator Zaffirini.

State senator Leticia Van De Putte in 2006. Courtesy of the Texas House of Representatives, Photography Department.

State representative Lena Guerrero and Governor Ann Richards in 1990. © Annie Leibovitz/Contact Press Images, courtesy of the artist.

Judge Elma Salinas-Ender in 2006. Photograph by T. R. Esquivel. Courtesy of Judge Elma Teresa Salinas-Ender.

Justice Linda R. Yañez in 2006. Courtesy of Justice Linda R. Yanez.

Chief justice Alma Lopez in 2006. Photograph by Al Rendon. Courtesy of Alma Lopez/Al Rendon.

Laredo mayor Betty Flores in 2006. Courtesy of the Laredo Mayor's Office.

Mayor Blanca Vela of Brownsville in 2004. Photograph by Gregory James Phelps © 2004.

Mayor Olivia Serna of Crystal City, far right, with (left to right) councilman Alberto Sanchez, Juan Hernandez, and Lady Bird Johnson, circa 1980. Courtesy of Diana Serna Aguilera.

Judge Mary Roman in 2006. Courtesy of Judge Mary Roman.

Dallas city council woman Anita Nanez Martinez at a Cinco de Mayo show in 1986.

*San Antonio city councilwoman Maria Antonietta Berriozabal and
her husband, Dr. Manual Berriozabal, at a Cesar Chavez ceremony
in 2004. Courtesy of Roberto von Ellenrieder.*

*El Paso city council-
woman Alicia
Chacón in 2006.*

Houston city councilwoman Graciela Saenz in 2006. Photograph by J. Thomas Ford © 2006.

Laredo city councilwoman Consuelo Montalvo in 2006. Courtesy of Consuelo Montalvo.

▓ ▓ ▓ ▓ ▓ ▓ ▓ ▓ ▓ ▓ ▓ ▓ ▓ ▓ ▓ ▓ ▓ ▓ ▓ ▓

CHAPTER 5

LATINAS IN STATEWIDE OFFICE

Lena, I think, is the epitome of what we're talking about when we say New
Texas. . . . Lena communicates an energy, a high level of involvement. Lena is
Hispanic, which will have a more and more dominant role in Texas in the near
future. She's . . . experienced, she's bright and she's Texan.

GOVERNOR ANN RICHARDS

INTRODUCTION

The Texas constitutional convention of 1869 intentionally designed Texas
government's executive branch as a plural executive in order to weaken
the role of the governor. The design was a response to an abuse of power
by Governor E. J. Davis following Reconstruction. Many statewide offices
that are appointed by a governor in a cabinet form of the executive branch,
such as those in other states or at the national level, are positions that
are elected statewide in Texas. Only the secretary of state is appointed by
the governor and considered a member of the plural executive. Although
governors in other states are considered the chief executive, most scholars of Texas politics consider the powers of the Texas lieutenant governor,
who is elected independently from the governor in a statewide ballot and
has strong legislative powers, to exceed those of the governor. In addition
to the governor and lieutenant governor, the state comptroller, attorney
general, agriculture commissioner, and general land commissioner are all
elected independently in a statewide ballot and comprise the plural executive. Four Latinos, but no Latinas, have served in the plural executive. Dan
Morales was elected to serve two four-year terms as attorney general from

1991 to 1998. Tony Garza (1995–1997), Alberto González (1997–1999), and Henry Cuellar (served one year in 2001 before resigning to run for the U.S. Congress) were all appointed by Republican governor George W. Bush to serve as secretary of state.

The executive branch is rounded out with several state agencies. All but two of them are led by individuals or multimember boards or commissions appointed by the governor with the consent of the Texas Senate. In addition, the governor has the power to make appointments to fill unexpired terms for some elected offices. The Railroad Commission and State Board of Education are the two executive agencies headed by elected bodies. Members of the Railroad Commission are elected statewide, and members of the State Board of Education are elected from districts.

The only Latina to serve in a statewide office in Texas was appointed by the governor to fill an unexpired term.[1] In January 1991, Lena (Elena) Guerrero was appointed by Governor Ann Richards to fill the unexpired term of John Sharp on the Texas Railroad Commission after Sharp was elected as the state comptroller. Since Guerrero, two Latinos, Tony Garza and Victor Carrillo, have also served on the commission. Guerrero's appointment was a strong statement by Governor Richards of her "New Texas"—a Texas where her appointments would reflect the state's demographic makeup. In the early 1990s, the Railroad Commission had regulatory authority over Texas's oil, gas, and transportation industries. When the state's economy relied predominantly on the oil industry, the commission wielded extraordinary power. However, the oil industry bust of the 1980s taught Texas to diversify its economy, lessening the dominance of oil and, therefore, the role of the commission.

This chapter focuses on Lena Guerrero. To understand her political ambition, we begin with her early exposure to politics and her decision to seek public office. We then examine her tenure as a member of the Texas House of Representatives and eventual appointment to the Texas Railroad Commission, and conclude with a description of her brief tenure on the commission and eventual electoral defeat.

POLITICAL SOCIALIZATION

Lena Guerrero was born November 27, 1957, in the Rio Grande valley town of Mission, Texas. She was the fifth of nine children, with ten years between herself and her next oldest sibling. According to Guerrero's older sister, Carmen, their parents were active in political and social causes; in her words, "It was politics and the church."[2] Their parents' political activism included paying other people's poll taxes and driving voters to the polls on election day, a practice their mother continued into her eighties. In addition, their family's home sits on a corner lot, providing a key location for campaign signs for as long as Guerrero and her sister can remember. Consequently, the Guerrero children were politically engaged, even if not active. Guerrero's parents also were involved in social activism that centered on the Catholic Church.

The early, unexpected death of her father, Alvaro Guerrero, at the age of fifty-one, when Lena was only eleven, changed the family dynamics. It forced Guerrero to grow up quickly and to participate in the upbringing of her younger siblings. Her father's untimely death also created financial hardships. Guerrero describes her mother, Adela, as "an unbelievably strong woman," and although she had never worked outside of the home, she found a job working in a school cafeteria in Mission. To supplement that limited income, the younger siblings, including Guerrero, traveled during the summer with their mother to the Texas Panhandle, where they worked in the agricultural fields.

Although Guerrero ran for several high school government positions and participated in Girls State, her goal when she left Mission to attend the University of Texas–Austin was to be a journalist. While majoring in journalism, she found an extracurricular outlet in the Austin political scene. During her undergraduate years she became an active member of the University Democrats, eventually becoming statewide president of the Texas Young Democrats (1979–1981). Her early involvement in Austin politics exposed her to some of Texas's most notable women. She worked on Carole Keeton McClellan's Austin mayoral campaign and Ann Richards's campaign for Travis County commissioner, and occasionally she worked for state representative Mary Jane Bode.[3] As a student, Guerrero helped Bode draft legislation that led to having a student representative on the University of Texas Board of Regents. Guerrero attributes her initial involvement at the capitol, and later interest, to her work for Representative Bode.

In just three years, 1980 to 1983, Guerrero advanced quickly. After leaving school in 1980 (despite not earning a degree), she became executive director of the Texas Women's Political Caucus. That same year she met Lionel "Leo" Aguirre, whom she would later marry, at a meeting of the Mexican American Democrats. Following her position at the Texas Women's Political Caucus, she briefly worked for the National Hispanic Institute. Then, with her business partners Richard Hamner and Gonzalo Barrientos (who was a representative for District 51 in the Texas House at the time), she founded Bravo Communications, a company that helped candidates target the Latino community.[4] In 1983 Guerrero advanced from employee to chair of the Texas Women's Political Caucus, managed the successful Austin mayoral campaign of Ron Mullen, and married Aguirre.

THE DECISION TO RUN

In 1983 Guerrero declared her candidacy for state representative of District 51 when Gonzalo Barrientos decided to vacate his house seat to run for the state senate. District 51 included the racially and ethnically diverse eastern portion of the city of Austin and Travis County. In fact, the combined Black and Latino population for District 51 was 46.6 percent, including people who identified themselves as both Black and Latino. Approximately 39.1 percent of the population identified themselves as Latino.

Although the open seat in a district with a significant Latino population provided the opportunity, Guerrero's decision to run was also influenced by her own ambition and the encouragement of others. She began the process by first consulting with her husband, and then with Barrientos about his decision to vacate his house seat to run for the Texas Senate. In her opinion, it was next necessary to approach "the leadership of the Latino males" in the Texas legislature, but Guerrero did not stop there: she also sought support from prominent Latinas in Austin, specifically those who might also be considering a run for the state legislative seat. Some of them already had committed to other candidates in the race, but others offered Guerrero their endorsement. Since the seat was open, her first race was very competitive. Guerrero believed it was her experience as Mullen's campaign manager that allowed her to "tap into the non-Hispanic business community and conservative money elements" in Austin (Trager 1987).

In the Democratic primary Guerrero faced five men, including two Latinos.[5] Since no candidate won a majority, Guerrero (who won approximately 35.7 percent of the vote) faced Brad Wiewel (who won approximately 23.9 percent of the vote) in a runoff.[6] She won the primary and was unopposed in the 1983 general election. In the 1986 and 1988 primary and general elections, Guerrero faced no significant challengers.

Upon her election as state representative for District 51, Guerrero became the youngest woman, at twenty-five, and only the second Latina, following Irma Rangel, to be elected to the Texas House. She served three terms, from 1985 to 1991, and during her tenure served as vice chair of the Rules and Resolutions Committee, the State Affairs Committee, and the Sunset Committee, and as a member of the Government Organization and Human Services Committee (Jones et al. 2000). Most accounts of Guerrero's first term in the Texas House, including that of her husband, depict Guerrero as an outspoken liberal who was not very successful. However, by her second legislative session, under the mentoring of Pete Laney (who later served as Speaker of the Texas House from 1993 to 2001), Guerrero learned how to work with her house colleagues to pass legislation. By the end of her tenure in the house, Guerrero was an established advocate of a variety of issues, passing legislation affecting groundwater management, child care, and teenage pregnancy (Burka 1989).

In 1989, during the 71st legislative session, Guerrero was named by *Texas Monthly* as one of their "Ten Best Legislators" based on her ability to win "the confidence of the people most likely to oppose her" (ibid., 88). She also won recognition from several groups for her work on environmental issues.

The previous year, Leo Jr. ("Little Leo") had been born. When asked how she was able to juggle her political career and family responsibilities, Guerrero credited her husband and his support. The difficulties of being a Texas representative, with long days during the regular and special legislative sessions, have often had negative consequences for women legislators, but Guerrero juggled familial responsibilities with her political ambition. Guerrero even brought Leo Jr. to the house floor at times so she could spend time with him.

ASCENDANCE AND LEADERSHIP IN THE TEXAS RAILROAD COMMISSION

During the late 1980s and early 1990s, Guerrero appeared to be quickly ascending in Texas politics, yet she remained a controversial figure. Her policy positions in the Texas House identified her as fairly liberal, although her political expertise gained support across the ideological spectrum. In 1990, Guerrero was selected as one of *Newsweek*'s up-and-coming Hispanic leaders and served as a campaign adviser during Ann Richards's gubernatorial race. She was often referred to as Richards's protégé, complete with bouffant hair and heavy Texas drawl. Once sworn into office, Governor Richards's first major appointment in 1991 was of Lena Guerrero to chair the Texas Railroad Commission, replacing John Sharp, who had been elected state comptroller. Guerrero became the first woman and the first racial or ethnic minority to serve on the one-hundred-year-old commission, but she had to begin campaigning as soon as she was appointed since her seat was up for reelection in 1992.

Long known as a "good ol' boys" club, the commission regulates Texas's oil, gas, and transportation industries, with which Guerrero was unfamiliar. Recognizing her lack of knowledge, Guerrero initially declined to chair the commission until she could become better educated, allowing the remaining two members of the commission to decide who should serve as chair. Guerrero was a quick study, spending time educating herself from atop oil rigs and meeting with industry executives. Once she felt more informed, she accepted her responsibilities as chair and began her campaign for reelection.

Just prior to her appointment on the Railroad Commission, one of Guerrero's former business partners described her as "a very strong and willful character" (Morris 1991). Such qualities were essential as she made her way through Texas's political web and managed some of life's more difficult moments over the next two years.

Guerrero had very little time to establish a record as a member of the Railroad Commission before her reelection campaign began. Although she faced minor opposition in the Democratic primary from David Young, she won the nomination with 59.67 percent of the vote. The Republican primary was closer. Barry Williamson (with 51.49 percent of the vote) narrowly defeated Carole Keeton Rylander (who received 48.5 percent of the vote) to gain the Republican nomination.[7]

After the primaries, it was evident that the general election campaign for the Texas Railroad Commission seat would be contentious. Because Guerrero spent little money campaigning against her lesser-known Democratic opponent, she had $1.1 million to spend in early September 1992.[8] Williamson had faced a more difficult and expensive challenge in the Republican primary, so even though he had raised an equivalent $1.1 million during the year, in early September he had only $212,000 in the bank (ibid.). Early polls showed the race as very close. One released by the *Dallas Morning News* showed Guerrero with a narrow lead over Williamson (35 percent to 29 percent), but with more than 30 percent of registered voters polled "undecided," and a margin of error of 3.5 percent (ibid.).

Williamson went on the attack, portraying Guerrero as a liberal career politician who lacked experience, while touting his own experience as an oil and gas lawyer, and his service in energy posts in the administration of presidents Ronald Reagan and George H. W. Bush. Guerrero emphasized her ability to bring opposing sides together, a skill learned in the state legislature, and tried to focus on her proposed Texas energy plan. She also pointed out Williamson's lack of Texas roots, and a conflict of interest through his wife's oil holdings (Hoppe 1992a).

In mid-September, the *Dallas Morning News* revealed that Guerrero had never graduated from the University of Texas–Austin. The article also stated that she had lied in a press release about graduating as a Phi Beta Kappa (an award not given to journalism students). Amidst accusations of lying, Guerrero resigned her seat on the Texas Railroad Commission but remained in the race. She was defeated in the general election, managing to get only 39.26 percent of the vote compared to Williamson's 53.65 percent.[9]

Experiencing such a public flogging might prompt others to disappear into the private sector, but Guerrero remained involved in politics. In 1993 she registered as a lobbyist to do what she had always done best: work the personal relationships in the Texas legislature. She also completed her degree requirements and formally graduated from the University of Texas.

Although this episode was a difficult stage in Guerrero's life, little prepared her for her current battle. In 2000, while exercising at home with a personal trainer, Guerrero collapsed with a seizure. Soon after, she was diagnosed with inoperable brain cancer. At the time, she was given six months to live.

Again, others might have elected to spend quiet, private time with family, but Guerrero plugged ahead, her tenacity evident in her decision to continue lobbying and remain active in the Austin political scene. At the time of her interview in 2004, her primary goal was seeing her son graduate from high school, which she did in 2006. She maintained her lobbying practice through 2005 and continues to encourage and mentor Latinas interested in public service. Seven years after her initial diagnosis, she continues to defy medical science.

CONCLUSION

The controversy that surrounded Lena Guerrero when she left the public eye has unfortunately overshadowed her contributions as a Latina trailblazer. The epitome of an ambitious politician, Guerrero ascended to statewide office as the result of intertwining factors. She pursued the political opportunities that came her way, relying on both formal and informal networks, and her experience is instructive for Latinas advancing through the political pipeline, particularly those who choose traditional paths of advancement.

Although Guerrero's political involvement in college appears to have shifted her focus from journalism to politics, two important influences should be noted. Her political life intersected with the lives of some of

Texas's most powerful men and women, individuals who became mentors and advocates for Guerrero as she pursued public office. She also established a strong network of women through her work for the Texas Women's Political Caucus. While these experiences certainly shaped Guerrero's political life, it is important not to dismiss the influence of her parents' political and social activism in priming Guerrero's political interests.

Guerrero's path was different from those of other Latina elected officials. Whereas other women profiled in this book made their way to elected office via community activism, Guerrero followed a traditional path through electoral politics to political office. Specifically, she was already politically experienced when she ran for the Texas Railroad Commission, having served in the Texas legislature and gaining recognition as an "up-and-coming" Latina. As a member of the Texas legislature, Guerrero learned how to compromise and work within the institution's structural constraints to become an effective policymaker, experience that she carried to the Texas Railroad Commission.

The most difficult lesson illustrated by Guerrero's political trajectory is related to one of the most significant challenges for Latinas interested in seeking statewide office in Texas: public scrutiny. Potential candidates should not dismiss the difficulties of such scrutiny, which can clearly take its toll. In addition, changes in party politics that began in Texas in the 1990s provided Republican candidates with substantial advantages. Nevertheless, according to the National Association of Latino Elected Officials, Latinas elected to state office who identified with a political party were more likely to identify with the Democratic Party. Therefore, positioning Latinas for statewide office in Texas will require soliciting and grooming Latina candidates who belong to the Republican Party, or finding a way to make the Democratic Party more competitive. The public scrutiny to which statewide office seekers are subjected and the change in party politics in Texas may explain why other Latinas have not been willing to pursue such positions.

■ ■

CHAPTER 6

LATINAS ON THE BENCH

> It would make sense why [there are so few Latina judges], because we have not
> been around long enough to be in the position to receive an appointment.
>
> CIRCUIT COURT JUSTICE LINDA YAÑES

INTRODUCTION

In October 1990, the *San Antonio Express-News* carried a story about "the conspicuous absence of Latinas on the Bench" (McGaffey 1990). The article identified only three in the entire state: district judge Elma Salinas Ender (Laredo), appointed in 1983, and county court-at-law judges Hilda Tagle (Corpus Christi), appointed in 1985, and Leticia Hinojosa (Edinburg), appointed in 1989 to a new bench post.

Close to fifteen years later, in 2004, the number of Latina judges had increased substantially, especially in Texas. According to a report by the American Bar Association's Task Force on Opportunities for Minorities, Texas led the country in the number of minority state and federal judges in 1994. In 2004, records of the National Association of Latino Elected Officials (NALEO) indicated that there were 70 Latina judicial and law enforcement officers in Texas, compared to more than 250 Latino officers. Among judicial posts in Texas, there were 7 Latina circuit court judges (with one serving as a chief justice) among the 80 appellate court justices, 12 Latinas among more than 400 district court judges, and more than 100 Latinas in other types of judicial offices, ranging from municipal court judges, county court-at-law judges, justices of the peace, city and county attorneys, and constables.[1] Notably, in 2004, of the six judges on the 13th Circuit Court (based in Corpus Christi and Edinburg), four were Latinas.

Thus, while Latinas have made great strides in recent years, as of 2004 they made up only 1 percent of the total number of Texas judges.

One of the three original judges on record in 1990, county court-at-law judge Hilda Tagle, was elected state judge in 1994 before becoming the first Latina from Texas to be appointed federal judge. She was appointed in 1995 by then-president Bill Clinton and confirmed in 1998.[2] As of 2004, she continued to serve as the only Latina federal judge from Texas. District judge Elma Salinas Ender was reelected in 2004 and continues to serve. County court-at-law judge Leticia Hinojosa—elected as a district court judge for an open seat in 1996 and reelected in 2000—served until she resigned the post to challenge U.S. representative Lloyd Doggett (D-Houston) in the March 2004 Democratic primary for the newly redrawn 25th congressional seat, a bid that was unsuccessful.

Part of the success of Latinas in the judicial arena can be attributed to the increasing number of Latinas completing law degrees. The Texas Bar Association, which tracks the number of Latina and Latino lawyers, indicates that as of 2003, 6.4 percent of attorneys in the state bar were Latino; of those, 66 percent were Latino and 34 percent Latina. In 2000, the state bar identified more than 1,150 practicing lawyers in the state with Spanish surnames. Latinas, however, still constituted less than 1 percent of all female attorneys in Texas, despite the increasing numbers of women practicing law over the last twenty years.

Nevertheless, as the number of Latina attorneys has increased, so has the pool of those eligible for judicial appointments. As noted in the chapter epigraph, a quote from one of the judges profiled in this chapter, the low number of Latina judges is not surprising because Latina attorneys have not been around long enough to gain the experience required for a judicial post. Historically, the legal profession and the judiciary have been dominated by white males.[3] Since Latinas have made a relatively late entry into the legal profession, and an even later entry into the judiciary, it is not surprising to see so few (McGaffey 1990).

With the exception of justices of the peace, a law degree is required to hold judicial office in Texas. It is also important to keep in mind that Texas requires state judges to be nominated in party primaries and elected in the general election. In fact, Texas is known to have very "politicized" judicial races, with campaign monies, especially from attorneys, strongly influencing the outcome of these races. District judges serve four-year terms and must have at least four years of legal experience; there are no term limits. Appellate court judges, who serve six-year terms, must have at least ten years of legal experience.

Equally important, it is common for district and appellate court judges to initially get their seat by gubernatorial appointment when vacancies occur or when new courts or court seats are created. Texas governors therefore have immense influence in shaping the demographic, gender, partisan, and ideological makeup of the judiciary. Some research suggests that racial and ethnic minorities, especially African Americans and Latinos, are more likely to become judges by appointment than election.[4] There is some evidence to support that conclusion here. Of the four Latina judges featured in this chapter, three were appointed to their posts, all by Democratic governors: one by Mark White and two by Ann Richards.[5]

As the eligibility pool of Latina lawyers increases, the number of Latinas serving as judges should increase as well. In fact, some observers believe that Latinas are in an excellent position for future appointments and successful judicial elections since women and racial/ethnic minorities often are viewed as more fair and impartial, giving greater attention to issues of equality than their male counterparts.

Another important aspect of the Texas judiciary is that until recently state judges were prevented from taking positions on issues, particularly during the campaign. The U.S. Supreme Court in 2002 struck down a Minnesota rule prohibiting judicial candidates from publicly discussing issues that come before the court, ruling that such prohibitions violate the constitutional right to free speech. That same year, the Texas Supreme Court lifted restrictions that had been part of the code of judicial conduct. Texas judges and judicial candidates now have the freedom to discuss issues as long as they do not comment on specific cases. Nevertheless, state judges, with few exceptions, are unwilling to take positions outside of official cases for fear that they may be viewed as biased. Consequently, unlike the other Latina public officials profiled in this book, these judges are restrained from taking positions on certain issues, and some simply refused to comment on particular issues. This stance also prevented them from taking strong advocacy roles. As one of the judges featured in this chapter points out, "Being a judge is so difficult at times because we are not allowed to take a position on anything."

The focus of this chapter is on state judges in district and appellate courts. The first Latino to serve on the Texas Supreme Court was Raul A. González from south Texas. The first Latino elected to a statewide office in Texas, he served from 1986 until 1999.[6] But there has never been a Latina elected to the two highest courts in Texas: the Supreme Court and the Court of Criminal Appeals. Circuit court justice Linda Reyna Yañes was the first Latina candidate to run, albeit unsuccessfully, as the sole

Democratic candidate for an open seat in a Republican-controlled Texas Supreme Court in 2002. She won close to 42 percent of the overall vote.

In this chapter, the first district court judges (the first appointed and the first elected) are examined, including the first appellate court judge, as well as the first Latina to serve as a chief justice on an appellate court. District court judge Elma Salinas Ender (based in Laredo) was the first Latina state district judge on record, appointed by then-governor Mark White in 1983 and elected that same year to the 341st District Court. She was born and raised in Laredo. On her father's side of the family, she is at least a sixth-generation Mexican American; on her mother's side, she is a third-generation Mexican American. Judge Salinas Ender has served as state judge for more than twenty years (Salinas Ender 2004).

In 1992, district court judge Mary Roman (based in San Antonio) was the first Latina elected as district judge, in her own right, in a countywide race in a major metropolitan area. One of seventeen women among forty-two judges, she is a third-generation Mexican American, born and raised in Corpus Christi, Texas. Judge Roman was reelected in 2004 and continues to serve as a state judge.

Circuit court justice Linda Reyna Yañes was the first Latina state appellate justice, appointed by then-governor Ann Richards in 1993 to the 13th Circuit Court, based in Corpus Christi and Edinburg. She is a sixth-generation Mexican American on her father's side of the family, and a third-generation Mexican American on her mother's side. She was born and raised in Rio Hondo, Texas, but spent periods of her life in Chicago. She was elected in 1994 to complete the remainder of the term and reelected in 2000 and 2004. She continues to serve on the 13th Circuit Court with three other Latina and two Latino justices as part of an all-Democratic bench presiding over twenty south Texas counties.

Chief justice Alma López was initially appointed in 1993 as an appellate court justice by then-governor Ann Richards to fill an unexpired term on the Fourth Circuit Court, based in San Antonio. She was born in Laredo, Texas, and raised in San Antonio. She is a fourth-generation Mexican American on her father's side. One of seven justices presiding over thirty-two south Texas counties, she was elected to the Fourth Circuit Court in 1995 and then reelected before being elected as the first Latina chief justice in 2002 to lead one of the fourteen circuits in Texas. In 2004, she was one of two female Democratic judges serving on the bench. Since 2005, she has shared the bench with five Republican women. When the sole remaining male judge was elected to the Texas Supreme Court in 2004, Governor Rick Perry appointed another woman to the bench in 2005, making it the only all-female circuit court in Texas until the November election in 2006. Governor Perry appointed Rebecca Simmons, a district judge from San Antonio, to the position (Hotchkin 2005).

Since there are still relatively few Mexican American women serving as judges in Texas, examining these women's backgrounds and ascendance to public office may bring us a step closer to answering why there are so few. To answer this question, this chapter focuses on four areas of inquiry: 1) political socialization, 2) their decision to run for public office and the barriers that they have faced, 3) leadership, and 4) representation and advocacy.

POLITICAL SOCIALIZATION

In addressing the political socialization of these Latina judges, it is important to note that in some respects they are different than most other Latinas in public office, primarily because they are highly educated. As mentioned earlier, a law degree is necessary to become a state judge in Texas. Three of these four women graduated from St. Mary's University School of Law in San Antonio; Justice Yañes graduated from Texas Southern University School of Law in Houston. Arguably, the law school experience of these women cultivated competitiveness, a strong work ethic, and assertiveness.

With respect to their personal lives, there are both similarities and differences. First, both district court judge Salinas Ender and Chief Justice López attribute their political socialization to their families, in particular to strong father figures. Judge Salinas Ender, for instance, described how she was raised in a family that regularly participated in campaigns and voting. Similarly, Chief Justice López described how her father was very politically active in his hometown of Falfurrias, Texas. She was fully immersed in politics at a very young age and became the first in her family to receive a law degree. She was also one of the first Mexican American women in Texas to receive a law degree. Later in life, as an attorney, she became very involved within the Democratic Party and served in several judicial campaigns as a treasurer or campaign manager.

In contrast, Justice Yañes's political awakening occurred when she was a teacher in south Texas. Her parents were migrant farmworkers, and she herself had picked cotton as a child. She quickly recognized the neglect and inequality that existed for immigrant children in the public schools. These issues spurred her interest in political campaigns within the Democratic Party, as well as La Raza Unida Party, in the early 1970s. In fact, she was fired from her teaching job because of her involvement with La Raza Unida. These issues and events politicized her.

Unlike the other three judges, Judge Roman describes herself as initially "apolitical." She admits that she was naive about politics. After deciding independently that there was an opportunity to run for an open seat, she found out that some of the older Hispanic attorneys in town had turned their backs on her, feeling that she should have asked for their support before making her decision. Running for office was really her first experience in politics.

THE DECISION TO RUN FOR THE JUDICIAL BENCH

As the literature suggests, the decision to run for public office can be very difficult, especially for women. The question remains whether the process of making that decision is any different for Latinas than for Latinos, other women, or other men. It should also be pointed out that unlike most public officials, judges are not, for the most part, in the public eye except during campaigns. That is not to say that a state judge cannot be propelled into the limelight, particularly if she is ruling on a controversial case with wide policy implications. Nevertheless, compared to other public offices, Texas judges are not as visible to the public.

Each of these judges was asked to describe why and how they decided to run for a judicial office. One notable characteristic, mentioned earlier, is that three of the judges were initially appointed, so technically they were running as incumbents, which gave them an initial advantage. Judge Roman was the only woman to run in the 1992 Democratic Primary, facing two male candidates for an open seat. She won in the runoff against an Anglo male opponent and ultimately beat her Anglo Republican male challenger. Since becoming a state judge, she has never faced an opponent. Her initial decision to run was reached after evaluating the political opportunity structure. Because this seat had been held by a Latino judge who was planning to retire, it was very likely that several candidates would enter the race. After realizing that none of the potential candidates had significant stature or name recognition, she concluded that she had a viable chance to win the election. Her motivation to run for this office stemmed from her legal work as an assistant district attorney and her focus on family law, specifically domestic violence. All she knew is, "she could do this."

In contrast, Judge Salinas Ender jokingly describes her decision to run as "being drafted." After receiving her law degree, she became president of the Young Lawyers Association, and when the state legislature proposed creating a new district court in her hometown of Laredo, she immediately got involved. Once it appeared that the court would be established, she began working to identify a qualified lawyer for the appointment, preferably a woman. Another female lawyer and friend suggested that Salinas Ender herself should vie for the position. She is quick to point out that she had no aspirations to be a judge when the opportunity was presented to her at the young age of thirty. But she could not pass up the chance to be not only one of the youngest appointed judges in the state, but also the first Latina judge. She also points out that having been involved in various community activities, she had a base of volunteers and supporters to draw from in her first bid for the office. Since becoming a state judge, she has never been challenged by an opponent.

Similar to Salinas Ender, Yañes was initially appointed to the circuit court bench; then-governor Richards made the appointment in 1993 to fill a vacant position. Justice Yañes had no judicial experience, but she had several years of legal experience working as an immigration lawyer and was director of the Immigration Project for Texas Rural Legal Aid. She had also established a strong national reputation as the attorney for one of the Texas school district cases, specifically that of the Brownsville district in south Texas. The cases were consolidated and ultimately appealed in the U.S. Supreme Court case of *Plyler v. Doe* (1982).[7] She recalls how shocked she was to hear of her appointment because she never had ambitions to become a judge. That initial appointment and the notoriety of being the first Latina appellate justice of Texas are among her most memorable experiences. She ran unopposed for the position the following year to complete the remainder of the term and ran again in 1998.

In 2002, Justice Yañes decided to run for the Texas Supreme Court as the Democratic nominee. Fortunately, she did not have to resign from her position as circuit court justice. Although she ran unopposed in the Democratic primary, she was unable to defeat her male Republican challenger. When asked why she decided to run for the Texas Supreme Court, she expressed how the work would be no different from her work as a circuit court justice, and at the time, all of the Supreme Court justices were from the same party, with not a single Hispanic on the bench. This perplexed her, given the state's population and demographics, and compelled her to run. As she points out, "Until there is an Hispanic on the Texas Supreme Court, there will not be anybody to challenge false assumptions or untruths, and . . . cases will be decided as though they have been properly analyzed, without different points of view at the table." She felt that it was absolutely necessary for the Texas Supreme Court to have the perspective of at least one Hispanic. In 2004, she was challenged for the first time by a Latina Republican, but she defeated her opponent in a close race, winning 52.8 percent of the vote.

Chief Justice López emphasized a political opportunity similar to that of Judge Roman. When the current chief justice, a Democrat, considered retiring, he expressed hope that she or her female Democratic colleague would consider running. This proposition was partly motivated by partisan politics, since there had never been a Republican chief justice, and the Fourth Circuit had become increasingly Republican. One of Chief Justice López's main concerns was going back on the campaign trail, having just come out of a grueling reelection campaign in 1999 facing an Anglo female challenger. Although she realized that going back out the following year to campaign for the chief justice position would be a big hurdle, she was motivated by the desire to continue the work of the Democrats, as well as to end her career on "this high note." When she asked her husband what he thought about her running for the position, he responded, "I'm ready." Her challenger, a male justice and colleague on the same court, at the end waged a nasty campaign against her. She nevertheless won the election in a close race.

BREAKING BARRIERS TO PUBLIC OFFICE

Most of the literature suggests that when women run for office, their chances are as good as those of men, particularly for open seats, and certainly as incumbents. Each of the judges in this study was asked whether or not there were any barriers they faced as candidates in general, or as Latinas, when running for a judicial office.[8]

As the discussion in Chapter 2 of literature on gender politics and Latina politics makes clear, family responsibilities continue to be a challenge for female candidates, especially Latinas. Cultural expectations require complete support and understanding from a candidate's family, particularly her spouse. The demands of the legal profession also require women to calculate to what extent public office compromises their familial obligations. Justice Yañes commented that she could not have accomplished as much as she had without a great family support system for raising her two daughters. Although her youngest was already in boarding school when she was appointed to the bench, Yañes still had to juggle her work schedule and family responsibilities.

Salinas Ender was not married when she was first appointed, but by the time she ran for her first term, she was engaged, and she jokes that she sent campaign literature along with her wedding invitations. During her first term, she married and had two daughters, who were still young children when she ran for reelection in 1987. Luckily for her, she said, she had a wonderfully supportive husband. Having children, however, did prevent her from pursuing higher office, such as the Texas Supreme Court. She says she would have been too concerned about who was going to be doing the car pool while she was at an out-of-town event, and she just could not see herself spending eighteen months away from her family. Since Judge Salinas Ender has never faced serious challengers, the decision to continue running for office has not been as difficult as for other candidates.

The experience of Judge Mary Roman, who raised four children, was quite different. She was a single mother in her thirties when she was an undergraduate, and she was in her forties by the time she earned her law degree. Although her children were grown and living outside the house when she ran for public office, she was still concerned about the amount of time her profession would take away from her family. As she points out, balancing work and family is always a challenge, but especially in the field of law because the work is very demanding. She also recognized that women, and Latinas in particular, tend to be more concerned about taking care of their families. These are concerns, she says, "that Latinas cannot actually set aside, nor should they be set aside."

Chief Justice López did not have children of her own, but she did help her husband raise his two children when she was a practicing attorney. By the time she was appointed an appellate court judge and considering running for chief justice, her stepchildren were independent adults. Although she had a very supportive husband, she says she still needed the full support of all of her close-knit, extended family, especially when she had to miss family functions because she had other obligations.

The judges were asked whether or not there were other factors, in addition to familial responsibilities, to consider in deciding to run for public office. As the literature suggests, raising campaign funds continues to be a challenge for female candidates, although this is beginning to change. It is unclear, however, whether Latina candidates have overcome this challenge. Culturally, women, and Latinas in particular, are socialized to avoid calling attention to themselves; instead, they are expected to always be humble and modest. Yet getting people and organizations to donate money requires candidates to convince them that they are worthy and viable candidates. As Justice Yañes points out, "I don't care what anybody says, women have a harder time raising money than men. It is just the way it is."

Despite the tremendous success of all four Latina judges, each expressed how difficult it is to raise enough campaign money, especially since judicial races in Texas are very costly. Interestingly, all four judges also pointed out that, for whatever reason, women ordinarily do not contribute money to campaigns. Unless this attitude changes, raising enough money for a successful campaign will continue to be an issue for all women running for office. Justice Yañes believes that most women don't have the money, and Judge Roman agrees: "Women just simply don't contribute . . . the type of money that men are willing to invest in political figures. We don't do that, and we don't have the money, and that's the problem."

All four judges agree that the difficulty of asking for money and raising enough of it were important challenges. A colleague of Justice Yañes said she would "rather be chewing glass than making a phone call to try to raise money. . . . Women don't raise the money the way men do, and I think it is because . . . we haven't . . . been in the world of money as long as men have." Raising money in such a short amount of time is also a challenge. As Judge Salinas Ender pointed out, she did not have access to "a room full of people in a country club, in one meeting, to raise that kind of money in such a short frame of time." Chief Justice López noted that men can cut deals on the golf course or in a bar, but not women. She also remarked that most Latinas come from humble beginnings, and only a few come from families willing to loan $50,000 or $100,000 for their campaigns. Some Anglo male and female candidates come from wealthy families who not only can lend them money but who also have enough influence to help them raise more. Clearly, Chief Justice López overcame these challenges. In fact, as an incumbent in 1999, and again in 2000 when she ran for chief justice, she raised more money than any other appellate judge in Texas.

As mentioned in Chapter 2, discrimination and stereotypes continue to hamper Latina candidates. Judge Salinas Ender, for instance, believes that there still is the perception that all Latinas are undereducated. She attributed that misperception, at least in part, to the current political climate. Justice Yañes pointed out that in south Texas Latinas have been very successful as judicial candidates, but racially polarized voting makes running for statewide office a different matter. Justice Yañes goes so far as to claim that "most Anglo voters will not vote for a candidate with an Hispanic surname."

Even internal cultural barriers continue to hinder Latinas interested in pursuing public office. As Chief Justice López noted, things are beginning to change, but many Latinas are still being raised to be "your typical, subservient, loving wife," making them "hesitant to step up to the plate" when it comes to public office. She also mentioned that lingering notion that a proper woman does not call attention to herself, and "you certainly never bragged. . . . [Politics] was a man's world that was not something women did." All four judges, however, were able to escape the restraints of convention, largely due to family support.

Other types of barriers were encountered by some of the judges. Judge Roman, for instance, pointed out the increased expectations by the public since there were so few Latina judges: "Because Latinas are still making inroads, Latinas on the bench must work hard to keep an excellent reputation so that those who follow in their footsteps would not be hurt in the process." Judge Salinas Ender pointed out the need for "a really tough skin," especially in the face of negative campaigning and blatantly false televised ads. Justice Yañes agreed, saying that having to face public scrutiny, as do all political candidates, can be difficult.

Interestingly, all four judges raised the point that being a Latina, particularly in San Antonio and south Texas, has been an advantage in recent years. Judge Roman contends that Latinas are very much accepted in her county. Judge Salinas Ender believes that if everyone would vote, we would have a lot more Latinas and Latinos in office. She pointed out that in her own experience, going door-to-door, she met many supportive men who "really didn't want the doors of opportunity closed to their daughters." Justice Yañes noted that Latinas who have won office in communities with heavily Hispanic populations received most of their support from Latina voters. As she put it, in those areas, "if you are an Hispanic woman, you are going to win." Chief Justice López claimed that female candidates in general have an advantage when running for judicial office, and that male candidates "quake when they get a female opponent."

Since all four Latinas featured in this chapter have had experience in judicial races, they were asked to offer advice to other Latinas interested in running for public office, and specifically for a judicial position. Their responses varied, but all felt that success was possible. Judge Roman advised Latinas interested in running for public office to "do their homework, understand who the political players are, be ready to ask for your family's support, and prepare, prepare, and prepare." Judge Salinas Ender pointed out that any Latina running for office should "just make sure that [she] wants it, that it's not because somebody else wants [her] to run. It's got to be you because you really have to give about 180 percent of yourself to run, and it's incredible the schedule you keep just in one county." She also noted that to prepare for the position, "you need to expand your political base." Justice Yañes suggested that Latinas interested in running for a judicial post should first get about seven years of legal experience to develop competence and confidence as a lawyer. Many candidates, she said, lack experience, and "you need to be a good lawyer before you become a good judge." Chief Justice López had only one piece of advice for future candidates: "just not to give up . . . there are so many groups. There are so many people out there that are willing to help. Certainly any Latina that would want to run for office, all they have to do is pick up the phone and call me."

LATINA LEADERSHIP

Given that these women were the first Latina judges and leaders within their community, each of them was asked to describe what makes a good leader. In describing their own leadership styles, most of these women pointed to the same characteristics that they viewed as important to being a good leader.

Three of the four judges felt that good listening skills are critical. As Judge Roman pointed out, "A good leader has the ability to listen, really listen and absorb what the person is actually saying," as well as the ramifications. Judge Salinas Ender also felt that strong listening skills are important for a good leader, but that they also had "to be able to bring these views to the table, respect these views, and then make the best decision possible." Chief Justice López also referred to good listening skills and noted that a good leader was one "willing to bend when necessary" to compromise.

Judge Salinas Ender pointed out that a sense of integrity is important. She also believes that a good leader must have a good heart as well as "a vision for their community and the betterment of their community." For Justice Yañes, a good leader is a consensus builder; as she put it, "someone who can bring diverse points of view together and motivate [people] to want to move to whatever that consensus is." Chief Justice López describes a good leader as "one who could show by example." She also believes a good leader needs to be a people person, "to view everyone as equals," and to "show respect for others."

The judges were also asked why there are so few Latina leaders. Justice Yañes attributed it to the fact that "Latinas are not being groomed and nurtured to be leaders." She pointed out how Latinas, especially, have "to overcome an entire psychological upbringing of being very submissive in a very paternalistic culture." Similarly, Chief Justice López remarked that the upbringing of most Latinas "does not encourage [them] to become leaders." As she put it, "People always have such low expectations of Latinas."

As Latina leaders themselves, they were asked to point out the most important issues affecting women in general, and Latinas in particular. Unsurprisingly, all consider access to a quality education one of the most important issues affecting Latinas, but they also cited health care, adequate child care, and equal pay.

REPRESENTATION AND ADVOCACY

Most political observers suggest that representatives' perceptions of their role greatly influence their style and effectiveness. One important aspect of being public officials with Mexican ancestry is how they identify themselves. Labels signifying ethnic ancestry vary, depending on many factors. These can include the geographic region, the level of political involvement (local, state, or national), and immigrant generational status. Two of the four judges prefer the term "Mexican American." Interestingly, these women have ancestral lineages in Texas of four or more generations. One other judge suggested that the label she uses for herself varies, but that she prefers calling herself a "Mexican." She also has an ancestral lineage of more than four generations as a Mexican American. Only one judge preferred the term "Latina." She indicated that she had started using the term recently, in part because she lives in a city, San Antonio, that appreciates the rich Mexican culture.

Another area of representation involves whether these Latina judges view themselves as feminists. As the literature suggests, most Latinas are reluctant to identify themselves as feminists for many reasons, but primarily because feminism connotes an identification with Anglo women. In this case, all four judges indicated that they consider themselves feminists, but each qualified the term. Although recognizing various types of feminists, one judge said she thought a feminist "stands for treating all persons with inalienable rights of dignity, of being human." She also recognized a transnational feminism, saying, "I have sisters in the world." Another judge preferred to define a feminist as "someone who believes that some men and some women are able to do certain things, and that you should have an opportunity to do what you are capable of doing." Another judge remarked that a feminist is someone who recognizes that "women have been discriminated against, have never been considered as equal to men. And until we become equal . . . I'm going to pull and push every woman I can to the forefront until there is equality." When asked how feminism was manifested in their public offices as state judges, most pointed to the importance of their work in family law and domestic violence, as well as children's advocacy.

CONCLUSION

All four of these women were trailblazers in many respects. They were often the first women in their families to go to college, the first to receive a law degree, and the first to hold public office. With respect to their political socialization, three of the four came from political families or were politically active early in their careers. It is important to note that only one of the Latinas featured in this chapter had aspirations to run for office. In fact, three of the four were initially appointed to their positions.

Although each of these women faced barriers when running for public office, they were able to overcome them. Most of them pointed out that when they were growing up, they never doubted that they could do anything they wanted to do. They were raised in supportive families and had their own supportive families, which was an essential component in deciding to run for public office. Equally important, three of the four women entered politics when their children were young adults, either in high school or living on their own.

All four women recognize that they hold positions of influence where they can affect people's lives for the better—in some cases, women's lives specifically. Ironically, as judges, their role as advocates is somewhat stifled since judges are not encouraged to be outspoken and opinionated. They all, however, exhibited strong feminist ideals, as well as a strong cultural identity. Finally, it is important to remember that Latina judges are still an anomaly in Texas politics. As mentioned, Latinas have made a relatively late entry into the legal profession, as well as the judiciary, and they are still not being groomed as leaders. However, as the eligibility pool continues to increase, Latinas are in a prime position to be important judicial policymakers. Latinas have the capacity to create change for all women, not just Latinas, in their roles as judges.

▦ ▦ ▦ ▦ ▦ ▦ ▦ ▦ ▦ ▦ ▦ ▦ ▦ ▦ ▦ ▦ ▦ ▦ ▦ ▦

CHAPTER 7

LATINAS AS MAYORS

I could no longer just stand by and see all the injustices being done. I felt that they needed to see their parents speaking up for them.   MAYOR OLIVIA SERNA

INTRODUCTION

This chapter examines the political biographies of three Latina mayors, all of whom are of Mexican American descent, one each from two of the largest border cities—Brownsville and Laredo—and one from a city with historical significance for Mexican American politics: Crystal City. Brownsville and Laredo were selected because they were the first major cities in Texas to have female Mexican American mayors; Crystal City was selected because of its historical significance to the Chicano Civil Rights Movement. It is important to note that as of 2007, no formal record existed of Mexican American women who have served as mayors in Texas. Also, although large cities such as San Antonio and El Paso have had Latina mayoral candidates, many have never elected a Mexican American woman as mayor. San Antonio has had two Latino mayors but has never elected a Latina. Likewise, Austin elected its first Latino mayor, Gustavo García, in 2001 but has never elected a Latina mayor. Nevertheless, within the past two decades, the state of Texas has seen an increase in the number of Mexican American women elected as mayors.

Why is the role of Latinas as *políticas*, as mayors, a relatively recent phenomenon in Texas politics? To answer this question and examine the impact Latinas have made, this chapter focuses on several areas of inquiry: 1) political socialization, 2) the decision to run for office and barriers that Latinas have faced, 3) Latina leadership, and 4) representational roles and advocacy. Since very few Mexican American women have held elected office as mayors, this chapter will conclude with some prescriptive possibilities for future generations of Latina leaders.

This chapter makes an important contribution to the study of women in Latino/a politics and Texas politics. First, it examines mayors from two sizeable border cities: Laredo and Brownsville. Both cities have a rich history influenced by the colonization of Mexico by Spain, the U.S.–Mexico War, and the Treaty of Guadalupe Hidalgo. Yet, in Texas, border cities are given the least amount of attention in state politics. These cities are also part of the poorest region in the state. Second, few studies have examined the election and impact of Latinas in local politics. Latinas (and Latinos) are most often elected in predominantly Hispanic cities, mostly in the border region, south of San Antonio.[1] Most of them are elected as municipal officers. Like other women, Latinas continue to be viewed as the primary caretakers, but becoming a mayor may be viewed as a natural extension of their traditional duties, and perhaps less threatening to the Latino community. Another explanation for the election of Latinas as mayors in certain cities may lie in the characteristics of the office of mayor and the type of municipal government.

The literature suggests that women are more likely to be elected in communities where political offices may not be desirable or prestigious. Municipal offices in Texas are often characterized as voluntary positions with low salaries or a small compensation. The city of Brownsville, for instance, pays its officers a nominal fee. Depending on the type of government, the mayor may or may not play a significant role as policymaker. In Texas politics, there are four principal forms of municipal government, with many variations: strong mayor–council, weak mayor–council, commission, and council-manager. Only home-rule cities (cities with a population of more than five thousand people) may decide which type of municipal government to adopt. Generally, the mayor presides over a council or commission.

Cities such as Houston have a strong mayor–council form of government. Brownsville has a commission form of government. In Brownsville, two of the six commissioners are elected at large, and the remaining four are elected in single-member districts. The most common form of municipal government, however, is the council-manager type. Cities such as Dallas, Austin, San Antonio, Laredo, and Crystal City are governed with this kind of system. Mayors are typically elected at large in nonpartisan elections. However, in some cities the mayor is elected at large every three years, and the mayor pro tempore is chosen by (and is a member of) the city council every year.

The mayor's functions and responsibilities may also contribute to the power of the office. Charters of most cities, for instance, allow the mayor to vote on any matter before the council; other cities, such as Laredo, allow the mayor to vote only to break a tie. It is also important to note that home-rule cities decide the terms of office and whether or not to institute term limits for its mayor. Term limits may make it easier for women, and Latinas in particular, to get elected. The city of Laredo has a four-year term for its mayor, with a two-term limit. Brownsville has a four-year term with no term limits, and Crystal City mayors serve a three-year term with no term limits.

In this chapter only three of the estimated seventy-five Latina mayors in Texas politics are examined: Blanca Sánchez Vela of Brownsville, Betty Flores of Laredo, and Olivia Serna of Crystal City.

Vela was the first female mayor in Brownsville, founded in 1848. She was the first of nine children born to Luis and Maria R. Sánchez.[2] A first-generation Mexican American whose parents had no more than a third- or fourth-grade education in Mexico, Serna was raised in Harlingen, Texas. She was married for forty-two years to the late Filemón B. Vela, a U.S. federal district judge. She has three children—Filemón Jr., Rafael, and Sylvia—and is also a grandmother. She attended Texas Southmost College (the former Kingsville A&I) and earned a Bachelor of Science degree as well as a Master of Education degree from the University of Texas–Pan American at Brownsville. Vela was a teacher and counselor before becoming the mayor of Brownsville in 1999. Vela served from May of that year until June 10, 2003. After only one term, Vela decided not to run for reelection. She felt she had dedicated 100 percent of her time to the office of the mayor and one term was enough for her. She never intended to run for a second term, believing that change is good and necessary.

In 1998, Betty Flores became the first Latina mayor of Laredo in its 240-year history. Mayor Flores is a second-generation Mexican American, born and raised in Laredo. She was reelected in 2002. She is also the first Mexican American woman to serve as mayor of a major city along the U.S.-Mexico border. In her second term, she presided over an all-male city council. She has had a long and distinguished civic career.

Unlike Brownsville and Laredo, Crystal City was founded by Anglos in the early 1900s. Located in an agricultural region, it was known as the "spinach capital" during the 1930s, and most Mexican Americans in the town were migrant laborers or cannery workers. Before the 1960s, all the political representatives in the community were Anglo. Influenced by the larger civil rights movement of the 1960s, Mexican Americans experimented with the concept of community control. Olivia Serna was one of the key players in the Mexican American quest to take control of their community and destiny at a time in American history when discrimination and racism were a way of life.[3] In 1979 she was elected to the city council, which then appointed her mayor. (In 2003, Crystal City changed the way it elected its mayors to an at-large system.) She served as mayor from August to November of that year, and again from April 1980 through 1982.[4]

Olivia Serna was born in Crystal City to Maria Del Refugio Coronado and Amado Coronado. Her mother was the city's first Spanish-speaking teacher, and her father was a community leader and one of the few Mexican Americans who owned a business (a slaughterhouse). As a second-generation Mexican American, Serna was one of the few Mexican American women to graduate from Crystal City High School in 1946.[5]

POLITICAL SOCIALIZATION

These three Latina mayors all first became involved in politics as adults. The literature refers to this as "counter-socialization" in adulthood—that is, a reorientation to politics occurring later in life. The involvement centered on their families and their communities, a characteristic that is consistent with the literature that suggests family traditions and cultural beliefs about helping others have a major impact in the politicization of Latinas.

Prior to becoming mayor of Laredo, Betty Flores had a 28-year career in banking. Initially a secretary, she worked her way up to become the first woman to serve as senior vice president in the Laredo National Bank's 106-year history.[6] Prior to her promotion, Flores worked extensively in the bank's business development section. Towards the end of her banking career, she became more involved in the community of Laredo. When she left banking, she worked for a community organization called the Aztec Economic Development and Preservation Corporation, a nonprofit group that constructs and rents housing to low-income families in Laredo. She first became involved in politics as an advocate for community development while working for this organization, when she began to learn more about the community's needs.

Blanca Sánchez Vela's initiation into politics began with her involvement in the campaigns of her family members. Her first exposure came when her husband decided to run for state representative in the early 1960s, and she became the chair of his campaign. The 1960s were politically turbulent times for Mexicanos in south Texas. Vela vividly remembers how the poll tax was used to keep Mexican Americans from voting. She knew it would be an uphill battle to get her husband elected, but they both believed that a change was needed because the "Anglo establishment" who controlled the city typically ignored the needs of its Mexican American residents. Although they ran a tough campaign, Vela's husband lost by two thousand votes. Nevertheless, she considered it a victory because the Anglo male incumbent, who had held the office for twenty-five years, did not receive 100 percent of the vote. Shortly thereafter, Vela's brother-in-law decided to run for county judge. She was chair of his campaign as well, and this time her candidate won.

After that election, Vela dedicated herself primarily to raising her children, although she remained active in the community. She was especially involved in religious activities, serving on the parish council, offering religious education to young people, participating in pre-marriage classes at the Catholic church, and being generally active within the Hispanic women's religious community. City politics was the furthest thing from her mind. Then, in 1983, she again became active in electoral politics when her eldest son, Filemón Jr., decided to run for city commissioner in Corpus Christi. As in the past, she immersed herself in the campaign. At the time Corpus Christi had an at-large system for electing its city commissioners. Given that Mexican Americans were a minority in the city, it was going to be another difficult battle. Her son lost, but came in fourth out of seventeen candidates in the general election. She then returned to Brownsville, but in 1989 her daughter-in-law, Rose, decided to run for a state district judicial position. Vela went back to Corpus Christi and campaigned once again for another family member, this time successfully. Her daughter-in-law has maintained the judicial post ever since and remains one of the few Latinas in judicial politics.

During the early 1990s, Vela's participation broadened from religious activities and political campaigns to business and civic activities. As she explains, these at first seemed foreign to her, and she found herself struggling to decide whether she should venture into this arena. In the early 1990s, for instance, Vela was asked to serve on the Public Utilities Board. She responded by saying, "Why should I? . . . I don't know anything about electricity, water. I have a master's in counseling. So that doesn't go with that." However, after some thought, and with the support of her husband, she told herself, "I better say yes. Because if I say no, what right would I have to complain that women are not serving on utility boards, or any other boards . . . so I said yes."

In addition to her work on the Public Utilities Board, Vela served in various roles for the Brownsville National Bank Board of Directors, the Development Board of the University of Texas at Brownsville and Texas Southmost College, the steering committee of the National Hispanic Scholarship Fund Committee, the Brownsville Public Library Foundation, and many other commissions. As these experiences broadened her knowledge about politics, she began to make connections between politics and important issues that involved her community. Her tenure on these boards and commissions gave her the opportunity to interact with local politicians and other government representatives, and she learned the importance of forming political relationships, as well as the art of compromise.

Unlike Flores or Vela, Serna's initiation into politics was largely shaped by the tumultuous period of protest politics and the Chicano movement of the 1960s and 1970s. She first got involved in politics during the Crystal City school walkout on December 9, 1969. Serna and her friends had personally experienced discrimination in Crystal City as they were growing up, but it was not until she saw that her own children were being denied their rights that she decided to stand up for them: "I could no longer just stand by and see all the injustices being done. I felt that they needed to see their parents speaking up for them." What had occurred was that one of her daughters, a senior in high school, got embroiled in challenging a discriminatory school practice. Her daughter and her friends were bothered that the school had only four cheerleaders and allowed only one Mexican American; the other three had to be Anglo. This unwritten policy existed despite the fact that 85 percent of the students were Mexican American, and only 15 percent were Anglo. Toward the end of the year a group of students began criticizing the way the school cheerleaders were picked and saying something should be done about it. To express their dissatisfaction, the students drew up a petition that also included other grievances. According to Serna, five girls took the petition to the high school principal. He apparently read it, said he could do nothing about it—that he did not have the authority—and that they had to go to the school district's superintendent. He then threw the petition in the wastebasket and told them it was "garbage." He also warned them that if they pursued their grievances, he would see to it that none of them would graduate in May. Because many of the students were seniors, and it was already March, they were faced with a dilemma. In the fall of 1969 students at the school initiated a complete walkout. By January of 1970 the school administration had given in to students' demands. The Mexican community was inspired and eventually gained control of the school board and the city council, paving the way for Olivia Serna's ascension to the office of mayor.

As the students were organizing, so were parents and other residents. José Angel Gutiérrez, a college student and activist, was working to mobilize Crystal City, and it was during this time that the community formed its own political party, La Raza Unida. The party's foundation stemmed from a community-based group called Ciudadanos Unidos (CU), a grassroots organization that La Raza Unida members had formed to address political issues following the school walkout (Navarro 1998). Olivia Serna was a member, as was her husband, José. At the time, CU was divided into two smaller, gender-based units. José was president of the men's organization of CU, and Olivia was one of the leaders of the delegation for the women of CU. Dissatisfied with this arrangement, many of the women, including Serna, demanded that the CU form one organization so that they could work together. Given that her husband was president of the men's organization, Serna was able to convince the groups to unite, but there were consequences (ibid.). After the women joined, the male membership slowly dropped, hurting the movement's momentum.

THE DECISION TO RUN AND BREAKING BARRIERS

Prior to Vela's bid for Brownsville's mayoral seat, she spent most of her married life involved with her family and her community. Her religious activity allowed her to reach out to children and families, a foundation that provided her with name recognition. Moreover, as mentioned, her involvement on various boards and commissions allowed her to develop and build a network among elite *políticos*.

Vela's decision to run for mayor in 1998 centered on conversations with family, as well as with friends from the various boards and commissions. Initially she was hesitant because although she knew how to run a campaign, she had never been a candidate. She had also decided to challenge the incumbent, Henry González, a Mexican American man who had held the office for eight years. She believed that he was out of touch with the families of Brownsville, and that she could do better. When her family and friends immediately threw their support behind her, she knew there was no turning back. She campaigned for a full year before the election. As she points out, she wanted the people of Brownsville to "really get to know her."

Vela's run for the mayor's seat was not without its share of obstacles. In one debate, the incumbent challenged her lack of experience in elective office. Vela responded, "I came from the volunteering field, not the political field. I want to be mayor so that I could listen to the elderly [and] to the young people; this is what I've done. I've walked South, North, East, and West Brownsville. My goal was to do as much as possible so people could see someone cares about them" (Booth 2003b). Vela emphasized her connection to the community and her willingness to improve the quality of life for the people of Brownsville.

Vela's role as a wife and grandmother also was challenged. At a Rotarian luncheon held weeks before the election, she and the incumbent discussed their campaign platforms before the audience. She proudly said that she had served as chairwoman of the city-owned utility board for eight years, and before that was a bank board member for sixteen years, and before that was a housewife raising three children, and that she was now a grandmother. Her incumbent responded that "it takes more than a housewife and a grandmother to be mayor in this city." Angered by his statement, Vela responded, "I don't understand him. . . . He's a grandfather himself. How does being a grandmother make me less qualified?" After the incident, Vela supporters wore T-shirts that read, "Housewives and grandmothers can be mayors" (Gomez 1999). Vela ultimately defeated the incumbent, winning 56 percent of the vote.

Many believe that that the incident at the luncheon galvanized women in Brownsville to support Vela. Others believe that just having a female candidate energized the election and increased voter turnout. Still, Vela's election may reflect a pattern in Brownsville that has become more evident in the past two decades. Since the city's first female city commissioner was elected in the late 1970s, two more women have served on the city commission. In the 1980s, several women won seats on the Brownsville school board. In the 1990s, the community for the first time elected a woman to serve on the board of the Brownsville Navigation District. In 2000, a woman was elected as district attorney for the first time, one woman was serving as a state district judge, and two women were serving as county court-at-law judges. In addition, the University of Texas at Brownsville/Texas Southmost College has had a female president for a decade, and a woman chairs its board (ibid.).

Unlike the election of Vela and Serna, Betty Flores's election stems from a long history of Latinas in electoral politics. Historians document that Laredo is one of the few cities in the state that has elected many Latinas to school boards, college boards, and county positions since the 1940s.[7]

While working for the Aztec Economic Development and Preservation Corporation in 1997, Flores learned that Mayor Saul Ramirez would not be running for reelection. Instead, he was going to leave office early to serve as President Bill Clinton's undersecretary of Housing and Urban Development (HUD). Slowly, candidates for the mayor's office began to surface—all men. Flores felt that some of the candidates were of questionable character, and she believed that Laredo deserved better. She thought about her own career and involvement in the community, and how much knowledge and experience she had gained during all those years in the banking business. She also thought about the network she had established over the years, and the advocacy work she had done for the city. Given her experience, she says, "I really started to think about [running for mayor] very seriously."

For Flores, the most important quality she felt she would need was confidence. Did she have what it takes to run a city like Laredo? She recognized that not having a college degree might be seen as a weakness; however, she did have twenty-eight years of banking experience. Over the years, she had developed networks in local, state, and national government, and she had spent years working in the community to make families stronger. She also had name recognition in the community. Flores finally decided that she had enough experience to help create a vision for the city and lead Laredo into the future.

Flores then met with a number of grassroots organizations and various friends who she thought would support her bid for the mayor's office. She even discussed the matter with then-governor Ann Richards at the 1997 National Conference of La Raza (NCLR). Governor Richards provided Flores with a list of things she should do and told her that she could count on her support.

Flores's husband was also important in her decision to run for mayor. She and her husband had married when she was seventeen and he was twenty. She recalls, "We promised each other that we would never go into politics . . . anything else would be okay." But something changed their minds:

> One day we were watching television and we learned that one more guy announced his candidacy for the mayor's office, and so my husband turns to me and says, "What's gonna happen to Laredo?" So, I just let that thought pass for a while, and then I turned to him and I said, "What do you think about me running for mayor?" And he turned to look at me, with this look on his face, and he said, "You know, I have been thinking the same thing."

It was at this point that she knew she could win.

Flores recalls that when she campaigned for mayor, she never made any promises. She was very "up front" with the people and would constantly say, "What you see is what you get." In 1998, in a special runoff election, the community of Laredo responded by electing her mayor with 55.39 percent of the vote.

One potential obstacle that Flores sees facing Latinas running for public office is their physical appearance. She contends that any Latina running for public office must be attractive, much more so than a white woman running for office; a Latina's physical appearance can either open the doors of opportunity, or make it difficult to get through them. Flores says she experienced this obstacle herself. When she was running for mayor, one of her male opponents, who said little about substantive issues, instead tried to make an issue of the fact that Flores smiled too much.

The familiar gender and cultural roles within the Mexican American community also make it difficult for women in politics. Flores claims that if her husband had not grown out of the idea that she stay home with the kids and not work outside the house, it would have cost them their marriage. Recalling the first time she went to work, she says, "When we got married, he was macho. He didn't want me to work. You know, [after] the day I started working, he wouldn't speak to me for months." But Mayor Flores has always embraced the role of a good wife, mother, and grandmother. She still makes dinner for her husband, insisting that she does it because she wants to: "He's my good guy. . . . He's the guy that's part of me, and has supported me, and is a part of my life. So I go make him his dinner, whatever he wants, because I want to do it." Flores makes it quite clear that her family is the most important commitment in her life, and everything else is secondary.

Serna first decided to run for office while she was immersed in the politics surrounding La Raza Unida and Ciudadanos Unidos. In the early 1970s, the CU organization became an influential and powerful political machine. However, by the mid-1970s, it had become factionalized and transformed into two smaller, competing political organizations, the Gutierristas, led by José Angel Gutiérrez, and the Barrioistas, led by Guadalupe Cortinas, as well as a social organization called El Barrio Club. The two factions were in constant political struggle, and this led to the demise of La Raza Unida Party (Navarro 1998).

Serna was part of the Gutierristas, and it was there that she learned to articulate her thoughts. She became an effective and confident speaker, and she was also one of the few in the community who could speak fluent English. Because her daughter was one of the three students that led the historic school walkout, Serna was asked to speak at community rallies in support of the walkout.

In 1976, Serna was asked by CU to run for the city council. She initially refused, but began contemplating the possibility. She knew that it would require total commitment and a great deal of time, as well as a tremendous amount of responsibility. She discussed it with her husband, and with his full support, she agreed to run for city council. At this point in their lives, they were heavily involved in the Chicano movement and felt there was no turning back. Serna's desire to run was rooted in the passion she had for her community: "I knew I wanted to make things better for the people in Crystal, especially for our young people, our hope for a better future. . . . I was very *animada* [inspired] because we were fighting for a good cause. I felt I owed it to my people and my six children to fight for our rights."

Serna ran for the city council on the Ciudadanos Unidos platform in 1976, but lost. She ran again in 1979, and this time won. She was then appointed by an all-male, all–Mexican American city council as mayor from August to November of that year and again from April 1980 through 1982.[8] She was the first female Mexican American city council member and mayor in Crystal City.

According to Serna, representing the community was by no means easy during those times, nor does she believe that it is any easier now. The barriers to representation are three-fold. As already mentioned, it takes a lot of money to run for public office, which for various reasons tends to be a challenge for Latinas. Second, to be effective, an elected official has to spend a lot of time at work. This can create hardships for the family, especially if a woman has children who also need a lot of attention. Third, women often lack self-confidence and have doubts about their ability to lead, in part because there are few female role models and mentors in politics. With these kinds of barriers, there also come risks. Serna explains it this way:

> Every time that a public official makes a decision, there is a risk that
> it might be misinterpreted and the official will be criticized for taking
> certain actions. Having to make hard decisions can also mean making
> enemies! The family needs to know that this happens in politics, and
> that they will have to live with that. There is also the risk for Latinas
> not being taken seriously by non-Latinos as being competent for the
> position. To overcome this stereotype, Latinas need to be very involved
> in their communities and have a significant track record to prove that
> they are just as capable as any other running for office, and that they
> have a clear plan of action for the work that needs to be done.

The experiences of Vela, Flores, and Serna are consistent with the literature on women in politics, which suggests that they are more likely to enter politics from community volunteerism or women's groups. Also, the experiences of these three women support the findings of scholars who study gender and politics: when asked to identify the top three risks for Latinas running for office, most participants point to financial burdens, invasion of family and personal life, and the risk of compromising values.

LATINA LEADERSHIP

Given that Vela, Flores, and Serna were the first Latina mayors and leaders within their communities, each was asked to describe the qualities of a good leader. In describing their own leadership styles, these women had varied responses, but working together was a common theme. The literature on women in politics asserts that women are more likely to share power and invite participation than impose dominance.

When asked how she would describe her leadership style, Vela explains it this way: "There are leaderships that have a pyramid. You have a top guy and it trickles down. Well, mine is like a pie type of leadership. Each piece of pie represents each commissioner. We need all of the pieces to make a pie. I need everybody's help. We all have to work together to get whatever it is we need to get done for the betterment of our community."

Vela believes that good leaders are sincere and humble. She has always believed in improving the quality of life for her community. The *Brownsville Herald* has described her leadership style as "a 'kinder and gentler' approach instead of submerging herself into the usual factions and tribal warfare of local politics. . . . Vela has worked quietly and steadily to build consensus on a City Commission with its share of egos and political ambition."[9] According to a political analyst from the University of Texas at Brownsville/Texas Southmost College, "Mayor Vela showed a willingness to deal with all segments of society. She was not tied to a faction as had been the case in the past. . . . She has established respect for women in local politics" (Booth 2003a). In 2002, Vela was awarded the OHTLI Award by the Mexican government through the Mexican consulate in Brownsville. OHTLI, an Aztec word, means "path," and the award recognizes people who work for the betterment of the Mexican community. Improving the quality of life for her community has always been Vela's goal.

Flores believes that being a good leader requires "dedication, commitment . . . truthfulness, especially truthfulness. If you're not true to yourself and the people you're trying to lead, you're not going to get anywhere.

Leadership is about making decisions, and leadership that affects other peoples' lives is the most crucial." She credits two people for having the greatest influence on her becoming the first Latina mayor of Laredo. The first is her father. She remembers him never treating her any differently than he did her brothers. Also, he supported not only her mother, brothers, and sisters, but also her grandmother and aunt, and he made the difficult decision to move the family out of the barrio to what became the first boulevard in Laredo. Her mother was the second most influential person in Flores's life. She recalls her mother as a strong woman who was nevertheless, at times, shy and insecure. Although brave enough to travel to Austin to take classes, the bus ride terrified her: "My mom would get on a bus and go to Austin to take classes . . . all the while she was trembling the whole way." Flores was inspired by her mother's experience, especially in times of doubt: "If someone who, on the inside, is so fearful and can do it, then I, who doesn't know that fear, can do it."

The one life-changing event that most tested Flores's strength was the death of her son in 1986 at the age of nineteen. She suddenly found herself in the role of a caretaker for her husband and daughter, but found she was able to be a source of strength for her family. Getting through this difficult period proved that she was emotionally strong enough to do a lot more than just raise a family and hold a steady job. Becoming mayor was not going to be too difficult for her. Flores models her leadership style after that of former governor Ann Richards. According to Flores, "Governor Richards had a way of telling people things that they don't like to hear, but she tells them in a way that they thank you. She was a leader that had compassion for the families of Texas."

Serna believes that a good leader must have a vision of how things should be and be able to get people to work together to accomplish those goals. Serna has always looked up to leaders such as José Angel Gutiérrez, Martin Luther King, Jr., and César Chávez. The CU, which was created by Gutiérrez, provided Serna with the opportunity to demonstrate to the community of Crystal City that she was strong and assertive, and that she could challenge the injustices to which Mexican Americans were subjected. Serna believes that women have always been treated as second-class citizens, expected to stay home and raise children. It has been even harder for minorities to be in positions of leadership. For Serna, politics is the process of creating change to improve conditions. To do this, she encouraged community input: "Politics and good public policymaking means involving the community and allowing them to participate." She recalls, "Our meetings were packed with people whose opinions were never listened to in the past." To this day, Serna is still remembered in the community as one of the best mayors the city ever had. She is remembered for creating housing for the poor, paving streets in all parts of the city, and implementing urban renewal projects that improved the lives of the poor.

REPRESENTATIONAL ROLES AND ADVOCACY

The literature suggests that how public officials view their role as representatives of their communities very much influences their style and approach to advocacy. One important aspect of being a public official, particularly for women, is whether they identify themselves as feminists. Although Vela, Flores, and Serna do not consider themselves feminists, they do exhibit gender consciousness.

In terms of their representational roles, these Latina mayors have the ability to serve as advocates and influence public policy. As the literature suggests, it is not unusual for female public officials to focus on policy areas that traditionally relate to women's issues and the family. One way to get a sense of how effective they have been as Latina mayors was to ask them to describe their most significant accomplishments. All three women were advocates for children, families, and their communities. Also of note is that their representative styles and priorities were largely shaped by the demographic makeup of their cities, as well as by regional politics.

Vela rejects the "feminist" label but considers herself a housewife and grandmother who is passionate about the issues affecting her community. When it comes to women's rights, she believes in educating men about the fact that "women can both reproduce and be in Washington." For Vela, the most important issue is education, given Brownsville's high rate of illiteracy. She also emphasizes the importance of having a university in the community. As she points out, "This makes it easier for those who graduate from high school to go to college because they don't have to leave home, and this keeps the cost of getting a degree down." She also believes that it is critical for Mexican Americans who get a college degree to go back to their communities and serve as role models to motivate young people and instill in them the belief that they can do anything they set their minds to. Vela has devoted her life to improving education for her community. She now spends her time speaking to various minority and Hispanic organizations, including the Texas Alliance for Minorities in Engineering, whose goal is to increase minority representation in occupations in which they have historically been underrepresented.

Health care, poverty, and unemployment are critical issues in the border region. Vela believes that more state money should be allocated to border cities, and that policies must be practical in order to be successful: "For example, in Brownsville, Levi Strauss employed a large number of Mexican Americans for twenty or thirty years. However, with the advent of the North American Free Trade Agreement, Levi Strauss closed. The state responded to the high number of displaced workers by retraining them, which required them to learn basic math and English." She has always wondered how it's possible to retrain workers who have only a second- or third-grade education in Mexico (which by American educational standards makes them illiterate) and teach them the fundamentals of math and English. As she points out, the policy needs to be more practical and provide the workers with jobs that are suitable to their skills.

Flores does not like to be considered a feminist either. As she points out, she does whatever she does because she wants to and is capable of doing it. For her, whoever is most capable should be the one to do something. She believes that if women want to compete and be taken seriously, they have to be well prepared. She believes that mayors should focus on what she calls "front door issues": family, health care, and education. As mayor of Laredo, Flores has been a strong advocate for families, and since 1998 her administration has assisted families in three areas: 1) providing first-time homebuyers with down payment assistance; 2) making funds available for housing rehabilitation; 3) and creating a number of affordable housing projects. Health care is also a family issue. Flores characterizes her position this way: "You've got to take care of families. Parents should not have to be faced with . . . you know, my baby needs his immunization and I only have ten dollars in the bank, or in my purse. Those are the real issues of the world, and the reality of the women and their families in Texas."

Flores also emphasizes the need for a strong education system: "No parent needs to worry about their kid being educated because K[indergarten] through sixteen is paid for." Her motto is "strong families make for a strong Texas." Her most significant achievement was ensuring that Laredo became the home of this country's only commercial bridge. In 2000, the International World Trade Bridge opened on time and under budget. According to Flores, the networks she had established over the years made the World Trade Bridge a reality. The second biggest accomplishment of Flores's tenure occurred in 2002 when she negotiated for Laredo's first major entertainment center. Laredo has also developed a diversified workforce that has dropped unemployment to record lows. It continues to be one of the country's fastest-growing cities, and has offices of seventy-four of the Fortune 100 companies. In addition, fifty-two countries conduct international trade via the Port of Laredo.[10]

Although Serna believes in women's rights and that women are just as capable as men, she says, "I don't agree with everything [espoused by feminists] because of my upbringing, but I do think we need more women to be in leadership positions." She does acknowledge that culture can be an additional obstacle for Latinas: "Latina women are taught to be in the background and let men make all the decisions in their lives. Consequently, many are very shy and embarrassed to speak their mind in public." When Serna looks back on her accomplishments as a leader, one thing stands out: "More women aspired for public office after the political experience in Crystal. Women now dominate public offices [there]. . . . My sisters are active campaign workers. Two of my nieces have served on the city council and school board." Serna also has two sons involved in public office: Roberto Serna was elected in 1991 as district attorney of Zavala, Dimmit, and Maverick Counties, and Eduardo Serna was elected county attorney of Zavala County in 2005.

Like Flores, Serna believes that the most pressing issue in Texas, and in the country, is education, and that quality education and equal opportunity should be the rights of every child. She also believes in the right to health care via Medicare, Medicaid, and the Children's Health Insurance Program (CHIP). Other important issues include equal pay for women, affirmative action, and simplifying the citizenship process for Mexicans already living in the United States.

CONCLUSION

The most challenging aspect of writing this chapter on the first Latinas elected as mayors was the lack of documentation. There is no official record or listing of Latina mayors in Texas, and references were practically nonexistent. The references that do exist sometimes have contradictory statements. Most of the information presented in this chapter came primarily from interviews and what few records the women themselves had collected and were willing to share. Nevertheless, documenting these women's achievements is critical for recognizing and preserving the record of Mexican American women's contributions to Texas politics and leadership.

Blanca Sánchez Vela, Betty Flores, and Olivia Serna are, without question, trailblazers. Their experiences provide a framework from which normative goals, as well as strategies for leadership, can be derived. All three women shared similar political socialization experiences. They were not recruited by any political party or community group but instead decided on their own, with some hesitation, to run for office. Second, the decision to run for office was made later in life, after they had established solid records in community involvement and their children were young adults.

Their participation in community service was critical to their political education and electability for three reasons. First, they learned how to be leaders. Vela served as director and chairwoman of several boards and commissions; Serna was a delegate in the CU; and Flores was a vice president of a bank and a leading figure in community development organizations. Serving in these various capacities provided training for their political careers and gave them opportunities to learn "to be political." Second, they were aware of the needs of their communities and the various issues that were most important to them. Third, working in the community permitted them to forge networks that later played a crucial role in fund-raising and policymaking. In fact, those networks often became the determining factor in deciding to run for mayor.

The second area of inquiry addresses how they decided to run for office and the barriers they faced. For Vela, Flores, and Serna, maintaining healthy relationships with their husbands was important. Before deciding to run for mayor, they each contemplated what the decision would mean for their spouses, who in each case were supportive. In two cases, the husbands were also politically active. Family support was essential for all three women during their campaigns, and after their ascension into the mayor's office, their families remained their top priority. They entered politics only after their children were young adults, in high school or older, and they acknowledge that becoming involved in politics while their children were young would have been difficult.

In terms of leadership, the third area of inquiry, Vela, Flores, and Serna share a style that is distinctly Latina; that is, they believe in serving the community before self. None of them viewed the mayor's office as a stepping stone to higher office; instead their goal was to improve the quality of life for their communities. All three women worked with city councils whose members had huge egos and where relationships were often contentious. Once they assumed the position of mayor, these women were willing to compromise with council members to ensure a cohesive government, and egos were put aside. They were willing to share leadership responsibilities and, most important, they listened. They listened to the community, various interest groups, and governmental appointed and elected officials.

In regard to the final area of inquiry, they all faced obstacles in their bids to become mayor. Vela, Serna, and Flores all recognized that gender influenced their representational roles and their approaches to advocacy. They were faced with stereotypes about the role of women in politics, and they were prepared to deal with them. Each of them was challenged in ways that men would not be. For example, Vela was questioned why she, as a grandmother, would be qualified to be mayor. Her male opponent questioned her gender role and tried to make that the issue. Interestingly, their gender was not an issue to the women, but only to their opponents. All of them felt that they knew the issues as well as their male opponents, and more important, they believed they had better visions and plans of action for their cities.

In addition, the types of issues that each candidate thought were important were suggestive of a gendered agenda: improving the quality of life, strengthening families, ensuring access to health care, and providing quality education. These issues seem to speak to their gender roles as women and mothers, but focusing on issues naturally associated with their gender helped make them effective leaders at the local level. Their priorities were also shaped by the demographic makeup of the region and the location of the city. Both Flores and Vela were able to establish cross-border relationships with Mexico, recognizing the importance of geopolitical position in the aftermath of the North American Free Trade Agreement.

Finally, all the women struggled with their decisions to pursue public office. They each carefully considered whether or not they could do the job, and each faced a level of self-doubt. It is interesting to note that the women never questioned whether they could compete with the male candidates. They also never questioned their knowledge about community needs. Whatever self-doubt they may have had at the beginning was clearly not a factor once they were elected, and these trailblazers in Texas politics and Latina leadership have left an important legacy for those who choose to follow in their footsteps.[11]

CHAPTER 8

LATINAS IN LOCAL GOVERNMENT

Well, I'm not sure if you know, but I've held four elected positions.

ALICIA CHACÓN, EL PASO CITY COUNCILWOMAN

INTRODUCTION

The remarkable Alicia Chacón has held four elected positions—Ysleta Independent School District school board member in 1970, El Paso County clerk in 1974, City of El Paso council member in 1983, and El Paso County judge in 1990. Chacón is four times over a "first," having the unique distinction of being the first Mexican American woman ever elected to those positions.

In the previous chapters, we detailed how Latinas have made great headway in various levels of government and in different arenas of Texas politics. This chapter focuses on five Latinas that have made great strides in local offices in Texas. The chapter will unfold in the following way: 1) a brief biographical overview of the five Latina firsts and their political socialization, 2) their decisions to run for public office and the barriers they confronted, 3) their leadership roles, and 4) their representational roles and advocacy in the community. Most political scientists agree that local government has a greater impact on people than any other level of government. On a daily basis, individuals are touched by the services that local government provides: garbage collection, police protection, emergency response services, street maintenance, libraries, and parks and recreation, to name a few.

In the state of Texas, cities with a population of five thousand or more are considered home-rule cities, meaning they can select from four different types of local governments: strong mayor–council, weak mayor–council, commission (which has almost disappeared), and council-manager, which is becoming the preferred method. In Texas, city council elections are nonpartisan and take place in odd-numbered years. Council members are selected in single-member districts or at-large systems. Some cities, either voluntarily or because of voting-rights lawsuits, have changed from at-large systems to single-member districts. This has been instrumental in electing minority candidates. Houston's city council is comprised of fourteen members; nine are elected from geographic districts, and five are elected at-large. Several cities have institutionalized term limits. In Laredo, council members can serve only a four-year, staggered term with a limit of two elected four-year terms. The City of El Paso recently moved to staggered terms, and council members drew straws; some are serving two-year terms; others, four-year terms; and still others, three terms of two years each. However, there are no term limits in El Paso. In Houston, city council members can serve three terms of two years each. San Antonio city council members serve for two years and can serve no more than two full terms. Of the five cities discussed in this chapter, four have a council-manager form of government: Dallas, Laredo, San Antonio, and El Paso. El Paso residents voted in 2004 to change from a weak mayor–council form of government to a council-manager form. Houston has a strong mayor–council form of local government.

FIVE LATINA FIRSTS AND THEIR POLITICAL SOCIALIZATION

The most recent data available from the National Association of Latino Elected and Appointed Officials (NALEO) indicates that in 2005, 96 Latinas were serving in Texas as members of city councils.[1]

The five Latina firsts whose political trajectories will be discussed are: El Pasoan Alicia Chacón; Anita Nanez Martinez from Dallas;[2] Maria Berriozábal from San Antonio;[3] Graciela (Gracie) Saenz, a native of Houston;[4] and Consuelo (Chelo) Montalvo of Laredo.[5] These women were selected for this study because they preceded today's Latina *políticas* in local government in distinctive ways. Chacón, as mentioned previously, was four times a first, quite an achievement for any politician. In 1969, Martinez became the first Latina elected to serve on a city council of a major U.S. city. Berriozábal was the first Latina to be elected to city government in a minority-majority city. Saenz was the first Latina to be elected to the city council in the fourth largest city in the United States. Montalvo was the first Latina to be elected to city government in a community whose population is over 94 percent Mexican American; the fastest-growing city in the state of Texas, Laredo is also the second fastest-growing city in the United States.[6]

Alicia Rosencrans Chacón was born in El Paso and attended schools in the Ysleta Independent School District. Chacón remembers that her father had always been active in politics: in 1930, he ran for constable in the little town of Canutillo, Texas, and won, and her parents also had friends who were active in politics. In particular, Chacón fondly remembers Senator Ralph Yarborough, known as "the patron saint of the Texas liberals," who would visit their home. "He was talking to us like we weren't a bunch of kids, and he was talking to us as if we were adults. And we just felt so good! 'Cause you could feel his enthusiasm, and you could also feel that he respected you." She describes Senator Yarborough as "probably the longest time political associate that I had in my early years."

Alicia married Joe Chacón, a member of the El Paso Police Department, and together they ran a Mexican food factory, which the Chacóns would maintain over time. Their children, like their mother, attended schools in the Ysleta Independent School District. Chacón joined the Parent Teacher Association and eventually ran for a seat on the school board because she was concerned about injustices that she witnessed in terms of delivering quality education to predominately Mexican American children.

In 1978, President Jimmy Carter appointed Chacón to serve as the Small Business Administration regional director; she was the first woman in the nation ever appointed to serve in that capacity. After accepting that position, she began commuting to Dallas. That same year, Secretary of State Cyrus Vance appointed Chacón, along with ninety-nine other Americans, to the United Nations Educational, Scientific, and Cultural Organization (UNESCO). For personal reasons, Chacón returned to El Paso twenty months later and continued to work with her husband, who had retired from the police force to work in their business. In 1983, she was elected to El Paso's city council and served until 1987.

In 1969, Anita Nanez Martinez was the first woman and Latina elected to serve in local government in Texas, and thereby became the first Latina woman to sit on a major U.S. city council. She served in that position until 1973. Martinez was born in a predominately Mexican section of Dallas known as "Little Mexico." Her parents owned a small business. She attended local public and parochial schools. She always felt herself a leader in her neighborhood. Even as a young child she would organize games for other children. In 1939, when she was just fourteen, Martinez went door-to-door soliciting signatures to have the road she lived on, Pearl Street, paved. She worked as a civil service employee and an executive secretary prior to her marriage to Alfred Martinez, a local restaurant owner. After she married, Martinez joined the Women's Auxiliary of the Dallas Restaurant Association. While raising her four children, she still found time to volunteer with community and parochial organizations, the YWCA, and the Dallas Independent School District. Martinez maintained close ties to the business community and over time developed a strong affiliation with the Republican Party.

More than a decade later, in 1981, Maria Berriozábal became the first Latina to serve on the San Antonio City Council, a position she held for ten years. Born Maria Antonietta Rodríguez, she grew up in a family of six children and attended parochial schools in San Antonio. Her parents had migrated to the United States during the Mexican Revolution of 1910. She assumed a very important role in her nuclear family by helping her parents make important decisions, including financial decisions that affected the family. "I was fourteen, and I had a mission, and my mission in life was to help my father and mother so my sisters and brothers could all go to college." Berriozábal taught catechism, and one day a Catholic sister organized a group to go teach catechism in "poor neighborhoods." The irony was not lost on her: "We were so poor, but we went to poor neighborhoods to teach catechism." She fondly remembers this experience: "I remember how struck I was by the act of getting together with a group, and doing something together. I was fascinated with doing something with other people, and organizing. And I think that became an opportunity I could find to be with other people, and that to me is politics."

Berriozábal was very active in the Catholic Church and joined a variety of organizations, always working with women's organizations and assuming positions of power. When she was twelve years old, she read about Margaret Chase Smith, the first female U.S. senator; when she learned that Smith had been a secretary at one time, she decided to become a secretary herself. Berriozábal was also deeply inspired by the appointment of Pope John the Twenty-third and the changes promoted by Vatican II. She lamented, "I read that Christians had a responsibility to be out in the world, not only as ministers, nuns, [and] priests, but also as lawyers, and teachers, and public officials, and I remember when I read that, it was an incredible insight." Berriozábal was also deeply moved and affected by the assassination of President Kennedy, a Catholic and Democrat with whom she identified. "I was working at the Salvation Army as a secretary, and my bosses were all Republicans, and they said, 'You know, Mary (they called me Mary), your president is gonna get inaugurated, so why don't you go to the dining room and watch it on T.V.'" She did, and when she heard him say, "Ask not what your country can do for you, but what you can do for your country," it was a turning point for her. She recalls feeling "that is me, I have to do this." And so her political activism began. After she married Manuel Berriozábal, she began studying political science at the University of Texas–San Antonio, and she received her bachelor's degree in 1979. She remembers that her university experience included "learning more about politics, and learning more about democracy and our political system." The War on Poverty program allowed for the creation of community development corporations in which church groups were able to participate. Berriozábal says that she "became a poverty warrior" and learned about political involvement from the War on Poverty programs.

Gracie Saenz credits her political aspirations to her civics teacher, "who was very involved in local politics. . . . He was probably one of the first Hispanic Republicans in Houston. He got us involved in political canvassing and getting people registered to vote. My first introduction to politics was through this teacher." Saenz also remembers taking a class in Mexican American Studies at the University of Houston with José Angel Gutiérrez, a La Raza Unida activist and professor of political science. "I remember taking classes with him and thinking, you know, the ideology of the Chicano movement was a little too extreme for me, brown power, all of the different activist organizations. . . . My father always taught us that we had to respect authority and elders." In 1992, when she was working as an attorney, Saenz became the first Latina elected to the Houston City Council.

Consuelo (Chelo) Montalvo and her husband got involved in politics through their association with the League of United Latin American Citizens (LULAC). Montalvo was encouraged to work on committees and to run for positions within the organization. The couple attended city council meetings that sparked their interest in city government and politics. The LULAC experience empowered Montalvo to challenge decision makers and elected officials. Her husband, John Peter Montalvo, served on the Laredo City Council in the 1980s, and Chelo served on the Laredo City Council from May 1988 to June 2000. She was mayor pro tempore of the city in 2000. She was the first woman on the city council to serve two terms and was ineligible to run again due to term limits. Montalvo represented District 8, an area that she describes as having "a lot of people, poor people, that we have here, especially in our district. This is the oldest district in the city of Laredo, the downtown area." She was also involved in revising the city charter when Laredo switched from a strong mayor–council type of government to a city manager form.

THE DECISION TO RUN (ALWAYS AT SOMEONE ELSE'S BEHEST)

I never had aspirations for political office—it always sought me.

ANITA N. MARTINEZ

He [Judge Al Leal] was the one that started feeding me this. . . . We need leaders who are educated, who are wanting to do the right thing, who will serve our community effectively and not embarrass us . . . he set the seed in me.

GRACIE SAENZ

Public office is a noble endeavor, it is a beautiful thing. . . . I got very close to the people, very close, very attached to the idea that the relationship [between] a constituent and their elected official is very unique. It is unlike anything else.

MARIA A. BERRIOZÁBAL

There are some commonalities in these Latinas' decisions to run for office. Not one of them knew at the time that they would be making history—that, in fact, they would be the first Latina in that elected position. They only learned that they would be "firsts" after they were heavily involved in the electoral process. All five women reported that they decided to run because a person, a friend, or mentor asked them to do so, or it was suggested by a group of close friends or associates.

As mentioned earlier, Alicia Chacón attended school in the Ysleta Independent School District. In the 1970s, her three children—Carlos, Corinne, and Sam—also attended "the family school." But the school buildings had deteriorated drastically by the time Alicia proudly joined the PTA and became the organization's president. Several community members, parents, and teachers had complained to the principal and to the school board, but their complaints were never addressed, and school officials disregarded their telephone calls. They were totally ignored and felt disrespected. Chacón ran for a seat on the Ysleta Independent School District Board because, as she put it, "they asked me to run." Teachers, community members, and parents who were aware of the district schools' dilapidated conditions were angry at being ignored.

Even though the Ysleta school district was 80 percent Latino, not one Latino had ever served on the school board, and not a single principal in the district was of Hispanic descent. Chacón ran against a twenty-year incumbent, Jessie Gaunck. At first it appeared that she had won by a small margin. However, as the votes were counted, the names of fifty voters on the machine were not listed on the precinct roster. A legal battle ensued with the assistance of George McAlmon and a legal defense team from the Mexican American Legal Defense and Education Fund (MALDEF). Four months later, and after a special election was held, Chacón made history. When her victory was finally announced, she became the first Latina elected to serve on the board of the Ysleta Independent School District.

According to Chacón, she became known as a troublemaker: "I took it as a compliment. I always worked within the system. We needed to make a lot of changes." She started questioning hiring practices and suggested that Hispanic women be given the opportunity to work in leadership roles as principals and assistant principals. While serving on the school board, Chacón decided to run for county clerk in El Paso County.

In 1974, at the age of thirty-nine, Chacón again made history when she was elected to serve as county clerk, the first woman ever to serve as an elected official in El Paso County. She beat five other candidates in the Democratic primary and thought she was "home free" until Thea Savage, a native of Germany married to a World War II veteran, intervened in the proceedings. Savage, who had been defeated in the Democratic Party primary, announced that she would seek the post as a write-in candidate.[7]

The El Paso Times endorsed Alicia Chacón for county clerk. There were 140,000 registered voters in El Paso County. In the final analysis, 46,486 people cast votes in that election, and Chacón received 33,422 votes.[8] The turnout for that election was 33 percent, and Chacon received 72 percent of the votes. Recent voter turnout in El Paso had been between 9 and 14 percent. High voter turnout when Chacón ran for office may be attributed to the fact that after the Voter Registration Act of 1965 had been passed, voter registration campaigns focused their efforts on minority communities. The other important factor was the emergence of another political party, el Partido de la Raza Unida.

La Raza Unida, an activist third-party organization, had been established four years earlier, in 1970, to increase social, economic, and political self-determination for Mexican Americans in Texas. The party fielded several candidates for office in that 1974 election: at the state level, Ramsey Muñiz was running for governor, and at the local level, José Tinajero for county commissioner; Magdalena Cisneros for justice of the peace in Precinct 3; Ricardo Enriquez for constable in Precinct 3; and Jesus Viramontes for constable in Precinct 5.[9] Equally important, in the neighboring state of New Mexico, Democrat Jerry Apodaca became the state's first Spanish-surnamed governor.

Though Chacón embraced the Chicano movement and worked with

Willie Velasquez and César Chávez, she nevertheless joined the Democratic Party in 1957. She worked on the state steering committee for several candidates, including Hubert Humphrey and Jimmy Carter. From 1968 to 1974, she served on the Texas Democratic Executive Committee, the first Mexican American to serve in that position. She attended the Democratic National Conventions in 1972 and 1976, and the state convention numerous times.

In the case of Anita Martinez, it appears someone of prominence in the community admired her from a distance and asked her to run for office. Martinez received a phone call from a woman she had never met named Candy Estrada. She asked Martinez to consider running for city council at the suggestion of Bill Alexander, the attorney for the City of Dallas at the time. Alexander had told her that Anita Martinez would win if she agreed to run for city council. Estrada said she wanted someone who would represent Mexican Americans well. When Martinez mentioned the conversation to her husband, Alfred, his first reaction was, "Are you nuts, with all the things that you are doing?" However, Martinez felt that running for office would be a way to bring about needed change, and her husband gave her his blessing.[10]

It was an epiphany that inspired Berriozábal to run for office. She had been working as a secretary in the legal department at HemisFair '68. Her boss interacted with the strategists in San Antonio politics. Her secretarial duties included taking minutes at meetings. Since her boss was chairman of the local Democratic Party, she had the distinct advantage of recording minutes. "I remember that the things they talked about and discussed were things I would see in the newspaper the next day. And I would say, 'Wow! We were talking about this, just the three of us; now look, I read it in the paper.' So this thing called politics is really good. I wanted to learn about that because I can do things for my neighborhood, I can do things for my *comunidad*." She decided to run for office "because there was no reason not to." From the beginning of the campaign, she was confident that she was going to win: "I was just so sure. It was the right thing to do. I was so confident I was the right person." Berriozábal saw this as an opportunity to bring about change and self-determination for Chicanos in the community. She attributes her success to "the people who helped. A lot of them had never been involved in politics. They were the ladies who were active in the church, young people, children, women, and there was a kind of innocence about it." Her opponent in that race was a San Antonio police officer, Al Peeler, who was favored to win because he enjoyed the support of the city's political establishment (Franks 1987).

Gracie Saenz was not expected to win. She recalled that

> every single political consultant that I went to said that there was
> just no way. They would not even touch me in terms of helping me
> because I had no money, no name recognition, no political base, run-
> ning against an incumbent, Beverley Chapman [an African American
> woman], on a ballot with eight others and very little time to campaign.
> But, the persons that did help me were a judge by the name of Al Leal
> and his wife, Mary. Judge Leal's family had grown as an influential
> family in the Houston political scene. With their help, we organized
> a significant grass roots campaign.

At the time Saenz first ran for city council, some Hispanic political
activists filed a lawsuit against the City of Houston to do away with the
at-large seats. The established Hispanic power elite wanted to dismantle
the bifurcated council seats (nine single-member districts and five at-
large). They argued that since no Hispanic had won an at-large seat, this
could be seen as unconstitutional and a violation of the voting rights of
the Hispanic minority. Saenz was the only Hispanic candidate running for
an at-large seat and would be in a critical political position representing
the entire city of Houston. Her loss would have supported their arguments
for single-member districts, but her victory proved detrimental to their
case. Nevertheless, her victory allowed for further Hispanic involvement
because it proved that Hispanic candidates could have crossover appeal.
Given the astronomical growth of Houston's Hispanic population, the bifurcated system will probably make it easier for Hispanics to get elected to
the city council.

Saenz had a difficult race against an incumbent for the at-large council
seat in 1992. She made it through the first round, garnering 15.1 percent
of the vote to come in second, while the incumbent was able to obtain
40 percent. The runoff was going to prove pivotal since the political establishment and the funding resources were all betting on the incumbent. A
strong grassroots coalition, along with a focused and aggressive campaign
targeting the Hispanic community by one of the strong mayoral candidates, Robert Lanier, helped garner the requisite strength to get the vote
out. Even at that, it was not until a television broadcast of videotape showing the incumbent pulling Saenz's campaign signs that the race took a
turn in her favor. Ultimately the race was won by 50.4 percent of the vote
in the runoff, a miracle in the eyes of this Latina leader. Her narrow victory was secured by the support of mayoral candidate Bob Lanier and An-

glo voters, since the Hispanic voting populace was still only 7 percent of
the voter turnout.

In reflecting on her candidacy, Saenz recalled:

> Houston was faced with a Hispanic leadership void. I saw where the
> political elite were always trying to tell the community that they
> needed to have designated leaders that could speak for them. If there
> were any issues in the community that needed to be addressed such as
> education, health care, jobs, they would ask, "Who is your leader so we
> can speak with them?" And so every single important issue that came
> our way was trying to be funneled into the hands of maybe four or five
> individuals. And my question was, "Why is it that we have to have one
> voice, when they have so many voices in every single important insti-
> tution in existence, whether its health, transportation, economics, or
> education? And yet, telling us that we have to have but one voice? . . .
> and that was when I decided that I would run. Our community at large
> needed to know that we had many incredible, well educated, and well
> prepared Hispanic professionals ready to take on public service.

The November 1997 election was quite contentious for a variety of reasons. First, Houston mayor Bob Lanier could not seek reelection because of
term limits, and eight candidates vied for the position. In addition, Proposition A would continue (or, if it failed, end) the city's 1995 affirmative action
program, which had helped women and minority-owned businesses win
city contracts (with a 20 percent goal for inclusion). It was one of the most
divisive issues on the ballot. Furthermore, there were elections for the
Houston Independent School District, Houston Community College Board,
fourteen proposed state constitutional amendments, and a series of bond issues. On the eve of the election, the Reverend Jesse Jackson attended a rally
in support of Proposition A. He was recorded as saying: "Citizens of good
will in this city must see the value of inclusion; Houston is in a pivotal position to point the way" (Mason 1997). Since Houston was the fourth largest
city in the United States, the election received national media attention.

Saenz credits family, friends, former classmates, teachers, and other
community members for her electoral success. Her volunteers were known
as "Gracie's guerillas." She had a cadre of more than 150 volunteers who
"worked twenty-four hours a day" to get her elected. Because she did not
have much money, her strategy was to post purple signs all over Houston,
a metropolitan area that spans over 660 square miles. As her campaign
unfolded, she received donations from people as far away as Chicago.

Like the other Latina leaders profiled in this chapter, Montalvo ran for office because other people encouraged her to do so. Montalvo's husband had served on the Laredo City Council in the 1980s. During his tenure in office, Montalvo became involved in helping with his work, often taking messages from constituents for her husband. Subsequently, Montalvo felt that she could serve the citizens of the city because she had learned so much from helping her husband. While taking and relaying messages from constituents, she felt that she could really help people: "Sometimes they don't want to talk to him; they want to talk to me, because I'm the woman of the house. I understand the people, the parents, the housewife, because of the kids, because of the work. And they can talk more directly to me than to a man. And that's why people would encourage me . . . you need to run. We want you to run." One of Montalvo's major concerns was her speaking ability: "I'm not a very good speaker *porque* I don't speak that much English." Yet she ran against three other candidates, all men, and won, becoming the first Latina to serve on the Laredo City Council. Montalvo states that she was a "representative for the poor and the underprivileged people, that they don't have any money, they don't know what to do. So that's why I decided I wanted to be part of the city council."

All five women credit their family, friends, neighbors, and community volunteers for helping them succeed electorally. It is interesting to note that they all enjoyed the support of their husbands during their political careers. Berriozábal describes her husband as "very helpful and an extraordinary man." This kind of familial support bodes well for Latinas, many of whom have limited financial resources to run a campaign and rely extensively on human capital—community resources and networks—for their races.

BREAKING BARRIERS TO PUBLIC OFFICE

Because I defied every single political consultant's idea of "this is the way you run an election." I defied every single thing that they said. That they just basically told me that there was no way that I could ever win this election.

GRACIE SAENZ, INTERVIEW, JUNE 2004

When Anita Martinez and Alicia Chacón ran for office at the height of the Chicano movement, they were not only challenging the broader communities' political agendas, but also gender roles and cultural tradition, given that the women's movement was also gaining strength and momentum. In 1969, Martinez was running for a citywide, at-large district in a highly competitive election that would become a historic race. Frank Hernandez, a local attorney, filed for candidacy for the same city council seat as an independent, thereby effectively splitting the Latino vote into two factions, a departure from the previous experience of having only one Latino candidate for an office. Two Anglo candidates also vied for this position. The Citizens Charter Association backed Anita Martinez, who ultimately received 21,984 votes. Frank Hernandez received 5,950, and the two Anglos combined received 13,851.[11] The Citizens Charter Association also helped to elect African Americans to the city council. Another Latino candidate, Manuel Almagner, who ran for city council in another district, was defeated.

Martinez credits her victory in part to the Citizens Charter Association, for their financial support, and the Dallas Restaurant Association Women's Auxiliary, for helping get out the vote. In 1969, on Cinco de Mayo, an important Mexican holiday, Anita Martinez was sworn into office as the first Mexican American elected to the Dallas City Council. She remembers that after she began serving, her colleagues on the council told her, "Don't work so hard. You make us look bad." Only 2,500 Mexican Americans were registered to vote in the Dallas City Council election when Anita Martinez ran for office in 1969. However, a major increase took place in the 1970s, when nearly 10,000 Mexican Americans voted.

Chacón made history a fourth time when she became the first woman and Latina elected to serve as a judge for El Paso County, and the first Mexican American to serve in that position. She defeated Luther Jones, a popular, longtime El Paso politician who had also served several terms as a member of the Texas legislature. Chacón served as county judge until 1994, when she ran unsuccessfully for reelection. She was defeated by Chuck Mattox, a classic "good ol' boy rancher," who subsequently served only one term.

Chacón describes a broader connection to the Chicano movement, working with leaders such as César Chávez, Willie Velasquez, and Antonia Hernandez. Chacón was working not only on local issues; she was also committed to the broader cause. Throughout the 1960s and 1970s, she promoted a political agenda that would come to fruition through the courts—challenging at-large districts in the City of El Paso, the El Paso Community College District, and the Ysleta Independent School District. In 1983, Chacón ran for city council in El Paso and defeated the incumbent David Escobar. She served in that capacity until 1987, again making history by being the first Latina to serve on the city council.

According to Chacón, the nature of political campaigning changed over time. She reminisced about the times when candidates raised money by having dances and selling tickets, and even having bake sales. As she points out, "Now one has to be a great fund-raiser." Chacón lamented how election campaigns have changed: they "used to be more fun than they are now. . . . You had a lot more grassroots and community activities. You didn't rely so much on television. You relied more on community organizations and a one-to-one type of relationship." She went on to say, "We don't play golf. Women are not part of the network. We rely on the informal process." Chacón described her fund-raising efforts as nontraditional and mentioned that banks, lawyers, labor unions, and Mexican American individuals donated to her campaigns.

One of the barriers Chacón encountered was other women because she was a devoted Catholic and not pro-choice. "The choice should come before one gets pregnant," she asserted. Women's organizations were lukewarm towards her candidacy because of her stance on abortion. "It took a long time for women to trust me. In the beginning I had more men supporting me than women."

Saenz and Chacón agree that politics is a nasty business. Chacón made it a point to take female friends along to meetings and other political activities. "I was very determined to protect my image as a homemaker, and as a very straight person; and I have always been very religious, a spiritual person. . . . I didn't go alone, lest people think I was loose." Chacón went on to add that the other problem was that campaigns and politics become very personal, and very nasty, and very judgmental: "You expose your family totally to public scrutiny. Nothing about your life is private anymore. . . . It's a very difficult decision [to run for public office]." Saenz echoed Chacón's sentiment: "Stupid things happen to you when you are in public office. People become jealous, and you can't understand why they do what they do. People become mean. They become ugly, and they say things that are so wrong and such lies. So you've got to be ready for the fact that people try to shoot you down. They are going to try to belittle you."

Montalvo ran for office after she learned the ropes from her husband and obtained the self-confidence that she could do the job. Nevertheless, she also mentioned the negative aspects of campaigning. In particular, her greatest barrier was the fact that she had left high school after completing her junior year, and she felt that she was not a very good speaker because of her limited English-speaking abilities. What helped her overcome these barriers was the encouragement she received from a broad-based constituency.

Berriozábal and Saenz were elected to their offices in the 1980s and 1990s, respectively. Berriozábal decided to run for office after San Antonio had single-member districts in place. One of her opponents had grown up on the west side and had moved out to the suburbs, but returned to her home district to run for office. She was critical of that and declared, "To me that was an insult; it was about self-determination. So I was very sure that I knew the issues of my neighbors, and . . . I think that's what I remember, and how beautiful it was." In terms of fund-raising, Berriozábal stated that money was a big issue "because you're not gonna get money from the people . . . unless you prove that you're very safe, and that you're not gonna rock the boat" (Franks 1987, 66).

LATINA LEADERSHIP

All five of these Latinas have a strong sense of justice and principles that they embraced as they developed and matured as leaders. They all credit their parents for instilling in them the importance of working with and for others. Leadership to Chacón involves three main ingredients: commitment, discipline, and compassion. She also added that a good leader has to have a vision. Chacón mentioned César Chávez, Willie Velasquez, Antonia Hernandez, and Henry Cisneros as people she admired for having good leadership qualities. She described herself as starting out as "kind of like a PTA leader, [but] I turned into a Chicano leader."[12]

Chacón attributes the lack of Latina leaders to "family concerns." In many ways, she comes across as rather conservative and traditional when she speaks about children and parental roles. Yet she also conveys the message that women need to get involved in the community to create a better place for their families.

In describing her own leadership style, Martinez says, "I have a strong sense of justice and righteousness. People know I follow through and accomplish what I promise. I go to bat for people in need. They call me *cuero de baqueta* [leather skin]. I do not let what other people say bother me. When people say bad things about me, I just keep going if there is an opportunity to do good, to bring people along, and to create progress for others."[13]

According to Martinez, leadership also involves an important trait: "Perseverance does not know what the word 'no' means. Be a good judge of character. Take people's talents and strengths and charge them with something that they can accomplish. Be good at giving other people credit when something is accomplished. People will follow a leader if the leader has a clear path or goal, and everyone knows it will benefit the whole community."

For Berriozábal, family and religion were important components in her upbringing and helped hone her leadership skills. Her grandmother, a devout Catholic who became president of many church organizations, served as a role model and helped Berriozábal cultivate her own leadership skills. She also credits her family for teaching her about democracy: "What I have learned—not only in school—about democracy is that it's the people. I had learned it at home. I had learned it at church. I had learned it at school. It is like everything I had ever learned I was able to go with to public life as an elected official, and put all those values to work." She admires her father as being a good leader, as well as César Chávez, Mahatma Gandhi, Dorothy Day, Martin Luther King, Jr., and Eleanor Roosevelt. Berriozábal says that she gets "really excited" about doing things for other people: "I like to bring leadership out of people." However, she does point out that "it is difficult to be a brown woman if you are a very assertive brown woman. It's like we are allowed to excel just so much as long as we don't threaten anybody . . . our men can't handle it . . . they don't know what do to with us" (Franks 1987, 66).

Saenz says one of her leadership qualities is having "the gift of gab"— being an effective communicator: "I think I have a passion for people. I have a passion for justice." She went on to add, "I have loved people who have been always working side by side . . . good leaders are those that inspire others to do the best that they can." She believes that U.S. senator Kay Bailey Hutchison is a good national leader. Saenz also believes that her husband, a Houston police officer, is a good leader. She benefited tremendously from his experience as a police officer because she learned about what was happening in the streets. She was also able to see the needs of police officers, though she did have to walk a fine line so as not to appear to have a conflict of interest.

In Laredo, Montalvo was busy at work, and at her behest, major road improvements on the San Francisco–Xavier Road came to fruition, helping the area's residents gain access to a major thoroughfare. Montalvo credits her association with the League of United Latin American Citizens (LULAC) for cultivating her leadership role. She also learned the ropes, so to speak, from her husband, who was a public official. She remembers attending a city meeting and saying to herself: "I can do it. I can do it better than the other council members that were there!" She recalls, "They didn't say anything during the meeting, and I was thinking, 'Why don't you say something?' or 'Come on, do it for the people,' you know! That's the way that I would do it."[14]

Language and culture appear to have been important factors for all five women's leadership. Anita Martinez promoted Mexican culture through dance and cultural events. Alicia Chacón emphasized that one should "value cultural background," and that it is important to speak or at least understand Spanish. Saenz fondly remembers how her father, who was born in Houston but raised in the Mexican state of Michoacán, "encouraged in us the understanding of his family tree. Every year we would go back to Mexico . . . and see really how difficult it was. He grew up in the rural countryside without any of the modern conveniences, no running water, no electricity, no T.V. So each year it was quite an ordeal for us as kids to go back and see this." Saenz stated that being able to speak Spanish was important to her: "I was able to easily float in and out of my communities without a problem, from the barrios. . . . And the Spanish came in very handy on the international side." Having traveled extensively to Latin America on trade missions and interacting with high-level officials, Saenz says, "My Spanish has been definitely a benefit to me." Similarly, despite Montalvo's limited English abilities, she was able to successfully negotiate the political system in Laredo, a predominantly Spanish-speaking community.

Berriozábal sprinkles words of Spanish into conversations very comfortably, and it seems that she has great linguistic maneuverability. However, it should be noted that when she decided to run for mayor of San Antonio, some of her critics claimed that she could not win because "she has too much of an accent." That, of course, is shorthand for saying that she's too obviously Hispanic to win Anglo votes (Franks 1987, 66).

Martinez, Chacón, Berriozábal, and Saenz indicated that they are very religious and spiritual, and derive great strength from their respective faiths. According to Martinez, the day before her historic election to the city council in Dallas, "I prayed to God to let me win big, or forget it, because I am not going to get in a runoff. I was listening to the radio and I heard about the lines of people waiting to get their licenses at the records building. God sent me the story, so I went to the records building to campaign. I know I picked up a lot of votes that day" (Martinez 2004). Saenz credited her faith for keeping her grounded and, in a special way, holding her accountable to herself.

REPRESENTATIONAL ROLES AND ADVOCACY

All five women were stellar advocates of community issues. In many ways, they served as links between established power brokers and their constituents. Martinez scheduled meetings throughout the city of Dallas in order to bring elected officials closer to the community. She recalls, "I held town meetings to see what citizens wanted. People were not always friendly. Pete Martinez, an angry militant man from Little Mexico, . . .

I asked him to give me ten things that needed to be done." Remarking proudly on her successful bid for reelection, she says, "I even had the support of the most militant group, the Brown Berets." It is interesting to note that Martinez enjoyed the backing of people in the business community and the Republican Party, yet she was able to use her position to help her community. Martinez lists her two major accomplishments as saving Pike Park from private developers and building the recreation center in west Dallas that now bears her name. Martinez personally believes that her greatest impact on public policy has been in the area of human rights, as well as in promoting education among Latino youth.

Martinez's election to the Dallas City Council in 1969 quickly yielded results: major improvements in park and recreation equipment and programs, street lighting, sidewalks, and paved streets appeared in Mexican American neighborhoods. Mexican Americans were appointed to the city boards, commissions, and committees, and Mexican American police officers became visible at community meetings and schools. Environmental laws were enforced, and industrial air polluters whose emissions affected Mexican American neighborhoods were forced to install pollution control equipment or be closed down. Martinez initiated a series of town hall meetings around Dallas, thereby motivating local residents to become involved in their community, and likewise, at her behest, various city officials went to parts of Dallas that were home to the underprivileged, minorities, and poor. In 1970 she also pushed the city council to proclaim September 16 (Mexican Independence Day) as "Mexico Day" in Dallas. She proudly read the proclamation at the Pike Park Independence Day celebration. In attendance was J. J. Rodríguez, president of the Federación de Organizaciones Mexicanas. This event was also a first for the city of Dallas.

Chacón lobbied the federal government for funding to bring water to *colonias*, one of her major accomplishments in her tenure as county judge. She is also very proud of the fact that her successful bids for office led many other Mexican Americans to run for public office. She served as a source of inspiration to others, including Dolores Briones, who ran successfully for county judge in El Paso in the 1990s. Chacón says, "My breaking some of the barriers has left the door open for many more and created opportunities."

Berriozábal's father watched every single city council meeting on television and then provided her with analysis and suggestions. He provided great insight and strategies for her political work. One council member said, "Maria is an extremely aggressive woman. She can play pretty tough when she wants to. If given a chance, my feeling is that she would roll right over you, full speed ahead. And that is not just my perception" (Franks 1987, 66). Some critics claimed that she worked very closely with neighborhood organizations and that she would not play "deal maker." Berriozábal was also criticized for being overtly "pro-Hispanic in her politics," though she insisted that she did not know what that meant (ibid.).

It is clear that she enjoyed the support of people in her district and was very much in tune with their needs, because she lived in communion with the district. By all accounts, her overall tenure in the city council was positive. Although several neighborhood improvement projects were passed, Berriozábal was not comfortable talking about her achievements. Berriozábal also led the effort to create the $10 million House Trust Fund, which helps provide housing for low-income people and the homeless, and continues to provide federal and private funds for affordable housing. She fought against giving special-interest tax abatements to low-wage businesses, and also businesses that were being erected over the recharge zone of the Edwards Aquifer, San Antonio's only source of drinking water. She served on the Border Region Citizens' Committee that developed a consensus plan for a $2 billion higher education package that was adopted by the Texas legislature to settle a lawsuit brought against the State of Texas by the Mexican American Legal Defense and Educational Fund. The settlement brought money to San Antonio to help develop the downtown campus of the University of Texas–San Antonio and to support the University of Texas Health Science Center. It also created resources for the development of new universities in the border region. She served as a very active honorary chair of the San Antonio Independent School District bond issue, working successfully with community leaders in pressing for passage of the historic $483 million bond issue for the repair of dilapidated inner city schools.

In Houston, Gracie Saenz worked to establish after-school programs for children, and to expand parks and recreational centers to meet the needs of young people. She was active in promoting affirmative action contracting for minority businesses. Saenz describes herself as a conduit: others came forth with ideas, and she just helped channel them through. Among those ideas that she pushed forward were promoting bilingualism of city employees so that parks, transportation systems, the zoo, and the airport would contribute to the atmosphere of being an international city. She played an important role in promoting Houston as a city conducive to international trade. Saenz noted that "Houston is changing. Baseball fields are being converted to soccer fields." Saenz mentioned how people in Houston celebrated Chinese New Year and how increasingly diverse the city was becoming, including a diverse Latino population. The city is increasingly multicultural, and according to Saenz, "Houston now has one of the most diverse city councils in this country." But she says, "It wasn't about me. It never was about Gracie. It was about a community and the ability to work together and make things happen. . . . I'm glad that somebody else is now council member. Now we have to help . . . and that is good, . . . that is the way I think it should be in a democracy."

Montalvo credits her mother, who was very strict and *muy derecha* (very proper), for being a major influence in her life. And she describes her relationship with her husband as that of a true alliance and partnership: "I helped him and he helped me, and our kids, they were very positive and would help us out, too." While serving on the city council, Montalvo achieved many successes locally through the building of roads and access routes. She describes her role as that of "a representative for the poor and the underprivileged people, that they don't have any money, they don't know what to do. So that's why I decided I wanted to be part of the city." Her commitment to her constituency is genuine: "I was learning to defend the people, the underprivileged people, because that's what my barrio, my district in the city is." She defended her voting record publicly and always voted for the "people out there . . . that put me in here, in this position." Montalvo says that she did a lot of research before casting any vote, and she emphatically justified her positions: "I'm going to go out there and vote for all the projects, housing, all the things that the people need." While she served on the city council, Montalvo supported the completion of the Columbia and World Trade International bridges, which ameliorated the traffic congestion through the city of Laredo. She was the lone dissenter on a controversial vote to hire a consultant to seek out companies that would explore the possibilities of privatizing the Laredo International Airport.[15] She also voted to fire city manager Florencio Peña, saying that "the city manager does not have the scope or vision to get economic prospects for the city." Both Saenz and Montalvo emphasized the importance of doing one's homework before acting on an issue.

LIFE AFTER ELECTED OFFICE

After leaving office, these five candidates continued to contribute extensively to their respective communities. Inspired by her work with young Dallas Hispanics, Martinez founded the Anita N. Martinez Ballet Folklórico. She believes that the self-esteem of young Hispanics can be increased by raising cultural awareness and promoting their rich cultural heritage. The Ballet Folklórico is now a major institution in the Dallas region and, through her leadership and vision, is able to garner public funding, grants, and private donations. Incorporated in 1981, the Ballet Folklórico has won statewide, national, and international recognition and fame.

Martinez's political accomplishments led to an outstanding record of improvements in the depressed communities of west Dallas and Little Mexico. In 1972, the Zonta Club bestowed upon Martinez a service award for her "distinctly constructive volunteer contribution to Dallas." She had the opportunity to interact with high-level elected officials, including three U.S. presidents. In 1973, President Richard Nixon appointed her to a three-year term to evaluate the U.S. Peace Corps (Martinez 1999). Her first assignment was to travel to North Africa, the Near East, Asia, and the Pacific to evaluate the strengths and weaknesses of the Peace Corps. She hand-delivered her Peace Corps report to President Gerald Ford at the White House in 1976. In 1991, President George H. W. Bush appointed Martinez to serve a three-year term on behalf of the Department of Transportation to oversee the expansion of opportunities for small and minority- and women-owned businesses. It was a remarkable journey for a hometown girl from Little Mexico.

Martinez served until 1973, but her political efforts had a long-lasting impact on the city of Dallas. At her behest, the city council approved the building of a recreation center in west Dallas, and the council dedicated the building in her honor in 1976. The Anita N. Martinez Recreational Center became the most utilized center in Dallas. Martinez then spearheaded a $1.96 million Dallas bond campaign to have the center renovated and enlarged after she was out of office.

After her exit from political life, Alicia Chacón became executive director of the El Paso United Way, retiring from that position in January 2003. She has served on more than twenty-five boards and committees, and continues to work on behalf of the community of El Paso, including becoming president of the board of the Non-Profit Enterprise Center. Chacón stated that she was ready to give her husband, Joe, the traditional home life that was impossible when she was a high-profile community mover and shaker.[16]

In 1995, the Ysleta Independent School District inaugurated the Alicia R. Chacón International Language Magnet School, whose embraced vision declares that "All Alicia R. Chacón students will demonstrate civic responsibility while becoming lifelong learners and risk-takers in a multicultural society."[17] According to Chacón, the school teaches the "curriculum of the future . . . it teaches not only the language of other people, but the culture and traditions . . . as we move our country and the whole world moves to globalization, the schools are going to have to follow the model of having students understand that and respect those different cultures."

After her tenure on the city council, Berriozábal decided in 1991 to run for mayor, a race she did not win. When Henry B. González, the longtime Democrat who represented a large part of San Antonio in the U.S. House of Representatives, retired, Berriozábal decided to seek that seat; however, the winner in that election was Charlie González, the former representative's son. Berriozábal continues to work in her church as well as in community organizations, but she is taking a reprieve from grassroots politics. She mentors young women and continues to serve as a source of inspiration to other Latinas seeking public office.

Saenz, meanwhile, in addition to her dedication and commitment to her legal practice, finds time to volunteer in the community, at her church, and in Latino organizations. Her most recent endeavor is working on the establishment of the nation's first Hispanic-owned bank, Aquila Bancorporation, which serves the inner-city residents of Houston (Greer 2001).

After Montalvo left the city council, she unsuccessfully ran for county commissioner in 2001. The redistricting based on the 2000 census data drew lines that put her at a disadvantage. That race ended in a runoff in which she placed third. Montalvo's husband, a retired employee of the U.S. Postal Service, has continued his involvement in local politics, serving on the Laredo Independent School District Board of Trustees and becoming chairman of the Laredo Housing Authority. They have four children and six grandchildren.

Montalvo has also served on the HIV Advisory Consortium Board for the city, as well as on the Laredo Independent School District Crisis Committee. At a candidates' debate for county commissioners at a Kiwanis Club meeting, others were extolling their degrees and credentials, while Montalvo, having an eleventh-grade education, proudly stated that she is a "domestic engineer," a homemaker, who proved herself as a leader in government. She listed her accomplishments as having bridges built and getting tractor trailers off downtown streets.

CONCLUSION—"NEW LATINAS ON THE BLOCK"

Serving in local politics enables Latinas to work in other sectors of their communities that can have compounding beneficial effects in areas such as health care, culture, the nonprofit sector, the arts, and education.

Though Latinas have made great headway, there is still a long way to go. Predominately Mexican American communities such as San Antonio and El Paso have never had but a handful of Latinas elected to public office. Other major cities with a large Mexican American population have had minimal political representation by women. Austin, Texas, for example, has never had a Latina on the city council.

In sum and in closing, all five elected officials indicated a desire to see more Latinas run for office. Chacón encourages and mentors other Latinas who are considering running for office, telling them, "Don't be scared by the lack of money." Saenz warns future officeholders "to really have a strong fortitude and inner strength." Bilingualism is becoming increasingly important, and campaigning in both English and Spanish is becoming a necessity for all candidates.

It is important to note that these five Latinas were not selected or actively recruited by political parties, but instead cultivated their own networks and provided their own leadership training. This is a sad indictment of political parties, which are supposed to cultivate future leadership.

With regard to their political socialization, all five women indicated that their respective families had a major impact on their political socialization. Alicia Chacón's father ran for public office, and high-level politicians visited them in their home to discuss politics when she was a child. Maria Berriozábal credits her grandmother for showing her the importance of helping others. All respondents mentioned that their husbands were instrumental in helping them achieve political success. Chelo Montalvo was inspired to run for office by her experience helping her husband fulfill his duties as a city council member. Gracie Saenz stated that she was more responsive to dealing with crime and police department issues because her husband was a police officer and supported her throughout her political career.

One notable pattern with respect to their decisions to run for office is that not one of the candidates had a master plan to hold public office. They all reported that someone else encouraged them to pursue a political career. Martinez received a phone call out of the blue; Chacón, Berriozábal, and Montalvo received encouragement from their friends and family; and a judge presented the idea to Saenz.

Their friendships, extended families, and established networks helped them overcome barriers to running for office. Gracie's "guerillas," Chacón's friends and family, and Berriozábal's networks were all credited with helping them win elections. In spite of the hardships that they encountered, they all indicated that barriers can be overcome with persistence and perseverance as well as with the support of family and friends.

These five Latina leaders continued to assume positions of leadership even after leaving public office. It appears that they employed relational feminist principles by ensuring that they worked well with others to achieve their goals, which were all community oriented. Not one of the interviewees felt motivated by individual gains; rather, they were all interested in helping the community. They expressed the sentiment that running for office was not about fulfilling their own personal agendas, but helping their communities—including the broader Latino community.

As advocates these Latinas were able to bring significant improvements to their communities. Martinez was instrumental in improving neighborhoods in Dallas; Chacón advocated for the inclusion of Latinos in the electoral process; Saenz worked as an international ambassador for the city of Houston, raising the profile of Latinos; and Montalvo worked tirelessly for the poor in her district and raised awareness of the hardships that they endured.

All have left a legacy in their communities. Martinez has made a major impact in the cultural arena; Chacón continues to be a source of inspiration to women running for public office; Saenz is focusing on economic empowerment issues for the Latino community; and Montalvo has served on various community boards and commissions, constantly reminding Laredoans that there is a large minority population whose needs must be met.

Indeed, all five candidates are great models for others who aspire to political office at all levels, and much can be drawn from their experiences, successes, and achievements. It is the trailblazing paths of these five unique and historic Latina "firsts"—Anita Nanez Martinez from Dallas, Alicia Chacón from El Paso, Maria Berriozábal from San Antonio, Graciela (Gracie) Saenz from Houston, and Consuelo (Chelo) Montalvo from Laredo—that others will continue to follow, forging their own new horizons and furthering the Latina vision, community by community.

EPILOGUE

We opened this book with the notion that Latinas are often viewed as novices in the political arena. We learned numerous lessons from this cadre of Latina trailblazers in Texas. Notably, each of the Latinas in the preceding chapters challenges the view that Latinas are invisible in the political arena. Although this was a small sample (a total of fifteen women), each case study provides clear evidence of the integral role of these Latinas as the first generation in public office.

Throughout this book, we have addressed four areas of inquiry in an attempt to further understand the roles of gender and culture for women in public office. The first area addressed political socialization. We were interested in learning how these Latinas became socialized into politics, and how this process may have contributed to their running for public office. As mentioned in Chapters 1 and 2, female elective and appointive officials may emerge from any number of paths of socialization. While political socialization of Latinas may vary, we expected cultural elements to be consistently present and to emerge alongside politicization.

In the case of the Latinas in our study, some were exposed to political campaigns or political issues early in their lives. Some were raised in politically active families, while others were not political until they ran for office. The role of culture, however, was present in most of these women's experiences. As minority women, they were exposed to issues such as discrimination and inequality, and they were very cognizant of these issues as they pursued a profession of public service.

Another area of inquiry that was addressed was their decision-making process in running for public office. As mentioned in Chapters 1 and 2, many factors affect women's decisions to run for public office. Studies conflict on whether gender differences exist in the decision process. While women have overcome most obstacles to public office, we expected that the experiences of Latina candidates have been overlooked, and so we expected cultural influences to be present.

The paths to office for Latinas in this book varied. The decision to run for public office and barriers faced by most of these Latinas followed patterns we would expect to find among all women. A couple of the first Latinas in their respective offices found their way to public office through what might be considered a traditional route similar to that of other public officeholders who have advanced incrementally to higher levels of public office. Others entered public office by way of community, social, or church activism.

One thing is certain, the Latinas in our study were not socialized to consider running for public office; they were not groomed for public service and did not have political ambitions. Perhaps as important as the patterns and trends we have identified is what was notably absent. At least for these Latina firsts, the traditional recruiting institutions, such as political parties, were largely absent. Some political leaders—such as former governors Ann Richards and Mark White, and Governor Rick Perry—took the initiative in their gubernatorial appointments of Latinas. However, without a stronger commitment by political parties, the number of Latinas running for office will remain relatively small, particularly in statewide races and districts with large constituencies.

One common theme that emerged in this study was that most of these Latinas were asked by community representatives, colleagues, friends, and supporters to consider running for office. Another common theme was previous involvement in their respective communities, making it a natural progression to serve as representatives of their communities. Most benefited from this grassroots support. In addition, having the support of their spouses and extended families was a critical element in their decisions to run for public office or, in the case of appointments, accept a position. It also determined whether or not they decided to stay in public office.

Equally important, obstacles and barriers are still present for Latinas in public office. Similar to other women, Latinas continue to face financial burdens to support their campaigns. They also face familial restraints because they are expected to be the primary caretakers. However, for Latinas, this role of caretaker is magnified when one considers the role of culture. In addition, experiencing sexism is compounded when race and ethnicity are included in the picture. Most of the Latinas in this study had to confront stereotypes when others argued that they should not consider running and would not be taken seriously. They also faced accusations that they would not be able to juggle public service and caring for their spouse and family. Despite such barriers, these Latina public officials were able to succeed. In most cases, they were able to draw from the support of their families and communities.

The third area of inquiry relates to leadership. As mentioned in Chapters 1 and 2, gender differences are often present in leadership styles. Similar to most women, Latina leaders have a propensity for building consensus, inviting participation, and empowering others. Yet, for Latinas, certain cultural elements were also present, such as the strong connection to family and community. During the course of the interviews, we learned about the many important personal values these women reflect in their daily lives. In particular, a strong cultural identity was manifested in the importance of language, and many of these women shared how important their religion and having faith were to them and their families. They also demonstrated leadership traits that reflect their struggles as minority women with an awareness of both gender and culture. In this regard, the Latinas in our study demonstrated attitudes and perspectives shaped by these interconnected traits.

The last area of inquiry relates to representational roles and advocacy. Latinas, like most women, have demonstrated a propensity to advocate for women and families. But, in contrast to many other female officeholders, Latinas also advocated for issues affecting the Latino community. Their experiences as minority women affected by the intersectionality of gender and ethnicity reflect their worldview and their capacity to advocate for their communities. Their advocacy was especially important for the Latinas holding local offices and state legislative offices. Latina judges, however, while cognizant of these issues, were restrained from taking an activist role.

CONTRIBUTING TO A THEORETICAL FRAMEWORK

Part of our goal in this book was to formulate an encompassing theoretical framework for the study of Latina politics—in particular, Latinas in public office. We have demonstrated many of the underlying components addressed in previous research and have added other dimensions.

Similar to the conclusions presented in existing literature, we found evidence of an interconnectedness or overlapping activity among the Latinas in our study. A theory of Latina politics must include the interconnectedness of community activism and the political arena, particularly for public officials. Latinas serve as connectors for their communities. In addition, we found evidence that Latinas demonstrate a strong cultural identity, coupled with an emphasis on language and spirituality for some of them. Most of the Latinas in our study focused on policies that assist families, women, and the Latino community. They also demonstrated certain attitudinal characteristics as minority women, drawing strongly from their families and cultural networks. Equally important, we demonstrated that Latinas have the capacity to negotiate, form coalitions, and adapt to differing political contexts.

FUTURE PROSPECTS

It is interesting to note the different periods of time during which some of these Latinas were successful in their pursuit of public office. For example, a couple of the first Latinas began their careers in the 1960s and 1970s during the height of the Mexican American civil rights movement. However, most of the Latinas, especially those pursuing larger constituencies, were successful in the 1980s and 1990s. Another notable pattern is that the Latinas in our study emerged from predominantly Mexican American constituencies, either from south Texas or El Paso. While Latinas have made great gains in running for elected positions, they remain a small minority, and few and far between in many large, predominately Mexican American communities in Texas.

It is important to note that our study was centered in Texas, a state that has an important political context with a unique political culture. It remains a relatively conservative state, one that is resistant to change. Equally important, since 1998 the state has become increasingly Republican. With the exception of one legislator, all of the Latina legislators, senators, judges, and statewide officials have been Democrats. We can safely assume that most of the local officeholders also were Democrats, despite the fact that these races are nonpartisan. In 2006, the Democrats fielded for the first time a Latina, Maria Luisa Alvarado, for lieutenant governor in the November election; she received 37.4 percent of the vote, losing to the Republican incumbent. The fact that Texas remains a Republican state has important implications for the future election of Latinas, but given the increasing presence of Latino and Latina voters in the state, we can expect a greater receptiveness to and success for future Latina candidates.

One recent indicator of this greater receptiveness in Texas to Latina leadership is the July 2006 election of Rosa Rosales as national president of the League of United Latin American Citizens (LULAC). LULAC remains the oldest and largest Latino organization in the United States. Rosales, a longtime San Antonio activist and labor organizer, was the first female state director of LULAC and only the second Latina to be elected national president in the organization's seventy-five-year history. Supported by more than 70 percent of the delegates to the national LULAC convention, Rosales was singled out for her ability to work with all groups and for the strength of her conviction to continue serving the Hispanic community by raising LULAC to a higher level of activism. While our study has focused on Texas Latinas elected to public office, we should not overlook the important contributions of Latinas in leadership positions in political, grassroots, and community organizations.

The critical question in a study on Latina politics is: why is it important to have more Latinas? We have already noted that Latinas demonstrate the capacity to advocate for women and the Latino community. Importantly, they also have the capacity to advocate for multiple constituencies. In a representative democracy, our elected officials must reflect the changing face of our society, but they must also maintain a continual vigilance to advocate for communities lacking representation.

We close this book with a final argument regarding the importance of having greater Latina representation, particularly at this time in our political history. In a recent U.S. Supreme Court ruling, a Texas congressional district was struck down for effectively diluting the voting rights of Latinos, and the state was mandated to redraw it. Recent policy debates in Congress, including the protracted struggle leading up to the renewal of the Voting Rights Act and the ongoing conflict over proposed immigration policy reforms, highlight the need for greater representation of minority communities. These policy areas are critical to fair representation, as well as the freedoms and quality of life of persons of color throughout the United States. Meanwhile the marches and demonstrations that have taken place in cities and towns across the country in response to congressional action and/or delay on these matters are also testimony to the growing grassroots mobilization of the Latino community and other minority populations. Because Latina leaders prioritize serving the interests of these marginalized groups, because their prior experiences and socialization typically keep Latinas well connected to the people and needs of local communities, and, finally, because Latina leadership styles are best suited for building consensus and forming coalitions, their increased presence at every level of the policymaking process is needed now more than ever.

▨ ▨ ▨ ▨ ▨ ▨ ▨ ▨ ▨ ▨ ▨ ▨ ▨ ▨ ▨ ▨ ▨ ▨ ▨ ▨

TABLES—LATINAS IN PUBLIC OFFICE

As noted in Chapter 1, the existing databases were incomplete or inaccurate. We have attempted to list all the Latina public officials for these offices. However, we apologize if some women have been inadvertently overlooked.

TABLE 1. *Latinas in the Texas House of Representatives, 1977–2007*

Term	Name	City for District
65th Legislature (1977–1979)	Irma Rangel	Kingsville
66th Legislature (1979–1981)	Irma Rangel	Kingsville
67th Legislature (1981–1983)	Irma Rangel	Kingsville
68th Legislature (1983–1985)	Irma Rangel	Kingsville
69th Legislature (1985–1987)	Lena Guerrero	Austin
	Irma Rangel	Kingsville
70th Legislature (1987–1989)	Lena Guerrero	Austin
	Irma Rangel	Kingsville
71st Legislature (1989–1991)	Lena Guerrero	Austin
	Irma Rangel	Kingsville
72nd Legislature (1991–1993)	Lena Guerrero*	Austin
	Christine Hernandez	San Antonio
	Irma Rangel	Kingsville
	Leticia Van de Putte	San Antonio
73rd Legislature (1993–1995)	Diana Davila	Houston
	Yolanda Flores	Houston
	Christine Hernandez	San Antonio
	Vilma Luna**	Corpus Christi
	Irma Rangel	Kingsville

(continued)

TABLE 1. *(continued)*

Term	Name	City for District
	Elvira Reyna***	Mesquite
	Sylvia Romo	San Antonio
	Leticia Van de Putte	San Antonio
74th Legislature (1995–1997)	Diana Davila	Houston
	Jessica Farrar	Houston
	Christine Hernandez	San Antonio
	Vilma Luna	Corpus Christi
	Irma Rangel	Kingsville
	Elvira Reyna	Mesquite
	Sylvia Romo	San Antonio
	Leticia Van de Putte	San Antonio
75th Legislature (1997–1999)	Norma Chavez	El Paso
	Diana Davila	Houston
	Jessica Farrar	Houston
	Christine Hernandez	San Antonio
	Vilma Luna	Corpus Christi
	Dora Olivo	Rosenburg
	Irma Rangel	Kingsville
	Elvira Reyna	Mesquite
	Sylvia Romo	San Antonio
	Leticia Van de Putte	San Antonio
76th Legislature (1999–2001)	Norma Chavez	El Paso
	Jessica Farrar	Houston
	Vilma Luna	Corpus Christi
	Dora Olivo	Rosenburg
	Irma Rangel	Kingsville
	Elvira Reyna	Mesquite
	Leticia Van de Putte****	San Antonio
77th Legislature (2001–2003)	Norma Chavez	El Paso
	Jessica Farrar	Houston
	Vilma Luna	Corpus Christi
	Dora Olivo	Rosenburg
	Irma Rangel	Kingsville
	Elvira Reyna	Mesquite
78th Legislature (2003–2005)	Gabi Canales	Alice
	Norma Chavez	El Paso
	Jessica Farrar	Houston
	Vilma Luna	Corpus Christi
	Dora Olivo	Rosenburg
	Irma Rangel*****	Kingsville
	Elvira Reyna	Mesquite
79th Legislature (2005–2007)	Norma Chavez	El Paso
	Jessica Farrar	Houston
	Veronica Gonzales	McAllen

TABLE 1. (continued)

Term	Name	City for District
	Vilma Luna	Corpus Christi
	Dora Olivo	Rosenburg
	Elvira Reyna	Mesquite
	Yvonne González Toureilles	Alice

*Elected but not sworn in; resigned to become railroad commissioner 1/1/1991.
**Elected in a special election 5/1/1993.
***Elected in a special election 11/30/1993.
****Elected to the Texas Senate in a special election 11/10/1999.
*****Died before she completed her term.

TABLE 2. *Latina State Judges, 1983–2003*

Name	City	Year*
Circuit Court Chief Justice		
Alma Lopez	San Antonio (4th Circuit)	2002
Circuit Court Justices		
Alma Lopez**	San Antonio (4th Circuit)	1993
Linda Yañes**	Edinburg (13th Circuit)	1993
Nelda Vidaurri Rodríguez	Edinburg (13th Circuit)	1994
Erlinda Castillo	Edinburg (13th Circuit)	2000
Eva Guzman (R)**	Houston (1st Circuit)	2001
Dori Contreras Garza	Edinburg (13th Circuit)	2002
Elsa Alcala (R)**	Houston (1st Circuit)	2002
District Court Judges		
Elma Salinas Ender**	Webb County (Laredo)	1983
Mary Roman	Bexar County (San Antonio)	1992
Hilda Tagle***	Nueces County (Corpus Christi)	1994
Kathleen Olivares	El Paso County (El Paso)	1994
Leticia Hinojosa***	Hidalgo County (Edinburg)	1996
Migdalia Lopez	Cameron County (Brownsville)	1998
Cynthia L. Muniz	Maverick County (Eagle Pass)	1998
Bonnie Rangel	El Paso County (El Paso)	1998
Rose Guerra Reyna	Hidalgo County (Edinburg)	1998
Rose Vela	Nueces County (Corpus Christi)	1998
Nelva Gonzales-Ramos	Nueces County (Corpus Christi)	2000
Leticia Lopez	Hidalgo County (Edinburg)	2000
Patricia Macias	El Paso County (El Paso)	2000
Aida S. Flores	Hidalgo County (Edinburg)	2000
Juanita Vazquez Gardner (R)**	Bexar County (San Antonio)	2000

(continued)

TABLE 2. *(continued)*

Name	City	Year
Elsa Alcala (R)***	Harris County (Houston)	1999
Carmen Rivera Worley (R)**	Denton County (Denton)	2003

*Year that they first took office.
**First appointed by the governor in office.
***No longer a district court judge.
NOTE: Coauthor Sonia R. García compiled this table relying on the Texas Secretary of State Web site; the list does not include family district judges.

TABLE 3. *Latina Mayors in Texas Cities, 1980–2004*

Name	City	Year
Helen S. Gonzales	La Grulla	1979
Paula Alvarez (pro tem)	Kyle	1981
Helen S. González	La Grulla	1981
Olivia Serna	Crystal City	1981
Helen Gonzelez	La Grulla	1983
Norma Garcia	Mercedes	1987
Ann Guzman	Lucas	1987
Sandra Martinez	Kyle	1987
Mary Ybanez	Los Ybanez	1987
Norma G. Garcia	Mercedes	1989
Lupita Piaz	Sinton	1989
Mary Ybanez	Los Ybanez	1989
San Juanita Zamora	Alton	1989
Norma G. Garcia	Mercedes	1991
Maria Sanchez-Rivera	Crystal City	1991
Mary A. Ybanez	Los Ybanez	1991
Mary J. Lopez	Hondo	1993
Eva F. Medrana	Mathis	1993
Sharon Suarez	Willow Park	1993
Lupe A. Uresti	Rosenberg	1993
Gloria Vasquez	Natalia	1993
Severita Lara de la Fuente	Crystal City	1995
Linda de Leon	Arcola	1995
Ofelia Garcia	Progreso	1995
Eva F. Medrano	Mathis	1995
Mary Jane Nunez	Elmendorf	1995
Cynthia Oliveira	Benavides	1995
Margarita Rodríguez	Big Wells	1995
Gloria G. Vasquez	Natalia	1995
Mary Ybanez	Los Ybanez	1995

TABLE 3. *(continued)*

Name	City	Year
Andrea Calve	Lucas	1997
C. Connie de la Garza	Harlingen	1997
Nell Fernandez	Rhome	1997
Elizabeth Flores	Laredo	1997*
Lonnie Flores	Donna	1997
Helen S. González	La Grulla	1997
Rafaela Lerma	Robstown	1997
Diana M. Martinez	Poteet	1997
Cynthia Oliveira	Benavides	1997
Maria Elena Rodríguez	Encinal	1997
Juanita K. "Nita" Sims	Nolanville	1997
Alcee Tavarez	Presido	1997
Norma Tullos	Premont	1997
Blanca Sanchez Vela	Brownsville	1997
Ruberta C. Vera	Natalia	1997
Mary Ybanez	Los Ybanez	1997
Andrea Calve	Lucas	2001
Cynthia Canales	Benavides	2001
Diana Cortez	La Grulla	2001
C. Connie de la Garza	Harlingen	2001
Elizabeth Flores	Laredo	2001
Lonnie Flores	Donna	2001
Carolyn Gonzales	Woodloch	2001
Alma "Fritz" Green	Evant	2001
Delores Martin	Manvel	2001
Erminia Slaughter	Elmendorf	2001
Blanca Sanchez Vela	Brownsville	2001
Ruberta C. Vera	Natalia	2001
Mary Ybanez	Los Ybanez	2001
Dora Alcala	Del Rio	2003
Diana Cortez	La Grulla	2003
C. Connie de la Garza	Harlingen	2003
Nell Fernandez	Rhome	2003
Elizabeth Flores	Laredo	2003
Gloria Flores	Big Wells	2003
Alma "Fritz'" Green	Evant	2003
Mary Ann Obregon	Dilley	2003
Hortencia Ochoa	Ropesville	2003
Delores M. Martin	Manvel	2003
Adeline Pierdolla	La Vernia	2003
Anita Rodríguez	Yoakum	2003
Irene Romero	Indian Lake	2003
Irma Sanchez	Socorro	2003

(continued)

TABLE 3. (continued)

Name	City	Year
Norma Tullos	Premont	2003
Blanca Sanchez Vela	Brownsville	2003
Ruberta C. Vera	Natalia	2003

*According to the city secretary of Laredo, Gustavo Guevara, this year is incorrect. Flores's political career began in 1998.

NOTE: Since there is no reliable source that documents the election of Latina mayors, coauthor Sharon A. Navarro relied on the *Texas Almanac* (1980–2004) despite some obvious methodological shortcomings.

TABLE 4. *Latina City Council Members in Texas, 1983–2007*

El Paso City Council	
Alicia Chacón	1983–1985
	1985–1987
Barbara Pérez	1993–1995
	1995–1997
	1997–1999
Rose Rodríguez	1999–2001
	2001–2003
Elvia Hernandez	1999–2001
Vivian Rojas	2003–2005
Melina Castro	2006–present
Houston City Council	
Gracie Saenz	1992–1997
Carol Alvarado	2001–present
San Antonio City Council	
Maria Berriozábal	1981–1991
Yolanda Vera	1985–1993
Helen Ayala	1995
Debra Guerrero	1997–2001
Nora X. Herrera	2003
Delicia Herrera	2005–present
Elena Guajardo	2005–present
Dallas City Council	
Anita Martinez	1969–1973
Elba Garcia	2001–present
Pauline Medrano	2005–present

NOTE: Cities selected for the appendix were the ones included in the study.

■ ■

INTERVIEW INSTRUMENT

INTRODUCTION

As you know, we are writing a book on the first Latinas elected as public officials in the state of Texas. The themes we will be addressing are relevant to all public officials, all women public officials, and all Latino public officials. However, we believe that Mexican American women public officials, particularly the first ones elected to specific political offices, have a unique perspective. Accordingly, as we discuss the following themes, we hope that you will highlight for us your insights and perspectives as the first Latina elected to public office.

I. POLITICAL BACKGROUND

1. How did you first become involved in politics (was it a particular event, specific people or groups, specific issues or causes, certain role models)?

2. Generally speaking, how do you view the role of politics? Did you have a different notion of politics before you ran for office? How did that view/idea change after you were elected?

3. Why and how did you first decide to run for (the office you currently hold)? What do you remember most when you first ran for (the office you currently hold) and got elected?

4. Running for public office involves various considerations. What kinds of factors did you have to consider in running (for the office you currently hold)?

5. Would you say there are still barriers facing women, and in particular Latinas, interested in running for public office? If so, what are the three biggest barriers facing Latinas interested in running for public office?

6. Do you think there are risks (or costs) involved in running for office? What kinds of risks or costs? Do you think there are any particular or unique risks for Latinas running for public office?

7. Of all your life experiences, which one or two do you think had the greatest influence on your becoming the first Latina (office you currently hold)?

8. What person(s) had the greatest influence on your becoming the first Latina in this office?

9. Are you a member of any Latina-based organizations? Which ones? If so, did this (these) organization(s) have any influence in your decision to run for (the office you currently hold)?

10. Overall, based on your experiences, what is one piece of advice that you would offer to a Latina interested in running for public office?

II. PERSONAL SUCCESSES

1. We have collected information about your life experiences and from your service in public office (secondary information); are there any other important life experiences or accomplishments that we should know about?

2. What would you say are the top two accomplishments as a public official that you are most proud of?

3. On what area of public policy do you feel you have had the greatest impact?

4. Recognizing that there are real world constraints or limitations, where do you see yourself in five years? In ten years?

III. LEADERSHIP

1. What do you think makes a good leader?

2. Which three people do you consider good leaders?

3. What leadership qualities do you see in yourself?

4. How do you think your supporters or the people who work for you would describe your leadership?

5. As you know, there are few women political leaders and even fewer Latina leaders; why do you suppose that is?

6. Do you think the criteria for being a leader are any different for Latinas than other women, or than Latinos? If so, what is different? Why do you suppose that is?

IV. POLICY ATTITUDES AND IDENTITY

1. Given that there are many pressing issues in Texas and in the country, which three policy issues do you think are most important for women? for Latinas specifically? for all Latinos? Please explain.

2. What are your views regarding the following policy issues? What would you describe, in your opinion, are the benchmarks (or points of significance) for each of these policy issues?

   a. Civil Rights

   b. Women's Rights—Feminism

    c. Reproductive Rights

    d. Education (elementary, secondary, higher education)

    e. Health Care

3. One final question, this relates to identity. As you know, Latinos and Latinas in the United States use a variety of labels to identify themselves as part of an ethnic and/or racial group. Most of these labels vary, depending on a number of factors, such as region, local vs. national politics, historical contexts, or personal choices that carry ideological underpinnings best understood by the person making that choice. What term, or label, do you most often use to characterize your identity? Why do you prefer to use this term?

NOTES

In terms of the author ordering for the book, Sonia R. García is listed first because of her lead in the project. Valerie Martinez-Ebers and Irasema Coronado are listed next as part of the original collaboration. Sharon A. Navarro and Patricia A. Jaramillo are listed next in the order they were solicited to join the project. We recognize that we each contributed our share to the final product.

CHAPTER 1

1. Recognizing that the use of a particular label varies with region, politics, and historical context, the term *Latina* is used interchangeably with Tejana, Chicana, Mexican American woman, Hispanic woman, and Mexicana. We also follow the tradition established by Hardy-Fanta (1993) and use the term *Latinos* to refer to Latino males, and *Latinas* to refer to Latina females, while *Latino politics* refers to politics or power relationships associated with both genders.

2. The Patricia Madrid and Heather Wilson election results were delayed because both parties negotiated the "ground rules" for counting the 3,756 remaining ballots. Of those, attention focused on the 2,698 provisional ballots cast on election day by voters whose registration could not be confirmed by poll workers. The remaining 1,058 "in lieu of" ballots—cast by people who requested absentee ballots but said they never received them—also remained to be counted. Before the provisional ballots could be counted, election workers had to determine whether they were valid. In cases where workers could not positively confirm that a ballot was either qualified or disqualified, it was set aside—a possible source of contention if Madrid had been able to close the gap. The margin remained narrow, but Madrid declined to challenge. See Michael Gisick, "Counting of Final Ballots to Begin," *Albuquerque Tribune,* November 13, 2006, p. B1.

3. This trend holds nationwide. According to the Center for American Women and Politics, of the 1,665 female state legislators in 2005, 69 were Latina. Latinas

have been elected to state legislatures in seventeen states. The center's Web site can be found at <www.rci.Rutgers.edu/~cawp>.

4. NALEO 1985, 1995, 2005 and <www.naleo.org>. Note that NALEO data have limitations. We found some omissions as well as discrepancies based on our intimate knowledge of elected officials in certain cities. Absent any other data, we will use these figures despite the shortcomings.

5. Demonstrating the increasing attention to Latinas in politics, the Center for American Women and Politics at Rutgers University unveiled an exclusive Latina Web site, *Elección Latina*, in 2001 containing information on current Latina elected officials. This Web site can be found at <www.rci.Rutgers.edu/~cawp/Eleccion/home.htm>.

6. For these state comparisons, see Thomas Rivera Policy Institute at <www.trpi.org>.

7. The Institute for Women's Policy Research can be found at <www.iwpr.org>.

CHAPTER 2

1. A related work is Elsa Chaney's seminal study, *Supermadre: Women in Latin American Politics* (1979), which sets forth the notion that women equated public service with an extension of household management, and that they became *supermadres* of the nation by caring and nurturing the citizenry as they would their own families.

2. Elazar (1984) concludes that the characteristics of the moralistic culture did not weigh heavily in Texas. This subculture views government as responsive to its citizenry; political participation is highly encouraged, and tolerance is valued.

CHAPTER 3

The information presented in this chapter was obtained from archival records and telephone interviews with Representative Rangel and members of her staff. The author wishes to acknowledge and thank José Angel Gutiérrez and the University of Texas at Arlington Special Collections for allowing the author to use the transcript of Dr. Gutiérrez's interview with Rangel.

1. For a listing of all Latinas elected to the Texas House of Representatives, see Appendix A, Table 1. Rangel was not the first Latina to run for the Texas legislature. In 1964, Virginia Muzquiz was the first Latina candidate when she competed in the Democratic primary to be the party's candidate for state representative in Texas House District 3. Muzquiz did not win the primary but several years later successfully ran for county clerk in Zavala County.

2. Rangel 1996. See also "Conference Examines Women in Public Life" (1975).

3. Cotera 1977, 14, as reported in Gutiérrez and Deen 2000.

4. "Conference Examines Women in Public Life" (1975).

5. With the election of Lena Guerrero in 1984, there were finally two Latina legislators, Rangel and Guerrero, in the 69th Texas Legislature.

6. Sarah Weddington is a nationally known activist for women's rights who

first acquired a national reputation when she successfully argued before the U.S. Supreme Court in the 1973 case legalizing abortion, *Roe v. Wade*.

7. The self-selected Task Group included Rangel; University of Texas vice provost Ricardo Romo; University of Texas professors Gerald Torres (Law), Jorge Chapa (LBJ School of Government), Susan González-Baker (Sociology), and David Montejano (director of the Center for Mexican American Studies); University of Texas students Oscar de la Torres and Mariela Olivares; and the MALDEF staff attorney in San Antonio, Al Kauffman.

8. In 2003, District 43 was 25 percent rural and 78 percent minority (75 percent Hispanic, 2 percent Black, and 1 percent Other non-Whites), with more than 30 percent living below the poverty level, and 40 percent of the adult residents having less than a high school education <www.house.state.tx.us/members/dist43/escobar.htm>.

CHAPTER 4

This chapter is based on interviews with Senator Van de Putte (2004) and Senator Zaffirini (2004) conducted by Patricia A. Jaramillo.

1. Legislative Reference Library (2007) <www.lrl.state.tx.us>.

2. In 2002, Senator Van de Putte ran unopposed in both the primary and general election. Although she faced primary opposition in 2004, she won the primary with 82 percent of the vote, and the general election with 57 percent of the vote against Republican and Libertarian opponents.

3. The Texas Senate elected Senator Bill Ratliff as lieutenant governor on the eighth ballot, according to the minutes for the Committee of the Whole Senate.

CHAPTER 5

For the source of the chapter epilogue, see Hoppe 1991.

1. Other Latinas who have served in Texas's executive branch include Mary Helen Berlanga and Hope Andrade. In 1982, Mary Helen Berlanga (D) became the first Latina to serve on the Texas State Board of Education. Members are elected from geographic districts drawn by the Texas legislature. When Berlanga's term began in 1982, the board was an appointed body. However, Berlanga has been elected to serve since 1988, when the board became an elected body. In 2003, Esperanza "Hope" Andrade was appointed by Governor Rick Perry to the Texas Transportation Commission to serve a six-year term. The commission is responsible for directing transportation policy for the state and overseeing billions of dollars in highway spending.

2. We were fortunate to interview Lena Guerrero for this chapter. However, because of her illness, the interview by Patricia A. Jaramillo was not as extensive as our interviews with other Latinas included in this book, and our reliance on secondary sources is greater than in other chapters. We would like to acknowledge and recognize Lionel Aguirre and Carmen Guerrero for their willingness to provide additional information regarding Guerrero's political career.

3. It is notable that Carole Keeton McClellan (at one time Keeton Rylander

and now Keeton Strayhorn) would later switch to the Republican Party. She occupied a parallel role to Lena Guerrero as an adviser to Clayton Williams when Guerrero advised Ann Richards during the 1992 Texas governor's race. Strayhorn later became Guerrero's political rival when she filed in 1992 for the Texas Railroad Commission race, although she lost to Barry Williamson, the eventual Republican nominee, in the primary. Strayhorn was elected Texas comptroller in 1998, as a Republican, and while still serving as comptroller, ran for governor in 2006 as an Independent candidate.

4. Gonzalo Barrientos would later leave the company, and Lionel Aguirre would join.

5. The five other candidates included Lawson P. Roberts, Lee Polanco, Brad Wiewel, Paul Hernandez, and Roland Ortiz.

6. Unofficial vote tally from the 1984 primary and general election, Travis County. "Precinct by Precinct Returns," Texas Secretary of State, Archives and Information Services Division, Texas State Library and Archives Commission.

7. Texas Secretary of State, Elections Division <*http://elections.sos.state.tx.us/ elchist.exe*>, accessed November 29, 2004.

8. See the series of *Dallas Morning News* articles by Christy Hoppe (1992).

9. Texas Secretary of State, Elections Division <http://elections.sos.state.tx.us/ elchist.exe>, accessed November 30, 2004.

CHAPTER 6

The interviews for this chapter were conducted by Sonia R. García.

1. Research based on the author's identification of fifteen Latina judges as of September 2004. The names of all the Latina state and appellate judges are listed in Appendix A, Table 2. In November 2006, six more Latina judges were elected.

2. According to an essay by the Honorable Sonia Sotomayor, the first Latina nominated to sit on a federal appellate court in 1997 from New York, there were approximately 30 Latino and Latina active federal district judges out of 587 judges in 2001. In 1998, there were only 11 Latina federal judges, comprising only 1 percent. See Muñoz 2002a.

3. See Hurwitz and Lanier 2003. The authors attribute this pattern to formal and informal methods of discrimination. Women, and especially racial and ethnic minorities, were barred or discouraged from entering law schools. Recent statistics show women are outpacing men in law schools; however, racial and ethnic minorities are still underrepresented.

4. The American Bar Association noted this pattern in the 1980s. Hurwitz and Lanier (2003) note that there is no consensus about which judicial selection method increases racial diversity. In their study, however, they found that the eligibility pool argument applies to racial and ethnic minorities since there is still a relatively small pool of lawyers.

5. Of the Latino and Latina state judges that initially received their judicial

posts by appointment, most have been appointed by Democratic governors. Only a handful of judges have been appointed by Republican governors.

6. Two other Latinos briefly served on the Texas Supreme Court. Alberto González was appointed by then-governor George W. Bush in 1999 to replace Justice González, and Javier Rodríguez was appointed by Governor Perry in 2002, but was unable to win the nomination in the Republican primary in the same year. As of 2004, one Latino was sitting on the Texas Supreme Court; Justice David Medina was appointed by Governor Rick Perry in January 2004.

7. This landmark case, which consolidated multiple school districts, struck down a state law that prohibited illegal immigrant children from attending public school in Texas. The court held that an attempt to deny the children of undocumented immigrants the benefits of a public education violated the U.S. Constitution. See 457 U.S. 202 (1982).

8. See an essay written by the Honorable Francis Muñoz (2002b) in the *Berkeley La Raza Law Journal* for a discussion of the barriers she faced. She was the first Latina district judge from California, appointed in 1978 by then-governor Jerry Brown. Foremost on her list were economic barriers since she came from a working-class family; cultural barriers, as well as discrimination, were also listed.

CHAPTER 7

1. See Appendix A, Table 3, for a listing of some of these Latina mayors.

2. The interview with Mayor Blanca Sánchez Vela was conducted by Sharon A. Navarro on October 27, 2003.

3. I would like to thank Diana Serna Aguilera for her assistance in providing me with information (D. Serna 2004) about her mother, Olivia Serna.

4. "Olivia Serna Leads Parade," *Sentinel,* November 12, 1998.

5. Olivia Serna was interviewed by Sharon A. Navarro on April 6, 2004.

6. Mayor Elizabeth "Betty" Flores was interviewed by Sonia García on January 8, 2004.

7. See Cardenas 1998.

8. "Olivia Serna Leads Parade."

9. See "A Class Act," *Brownsville Herald,* April 27, 2003, p. E1.

10. See Laredo 2004.

11. Olivia Serna died on December 19, 2004, at age 77 of breast cancer. She was buried in Crystal City, Texas, where she was born.

CHAPTER 8

The chapter epigraph came from an interview conducted by Irasema Coronado on February 3, 2004. Chacón is the councilwoman's married name; she was born Alicia Rosencrans.

The section epigraphs in this chapter are from the interviews cited in notes 2–5.

1. NALEO Directory 2005. As noted in chapter 1, NALEO data have several omissions and discrepancies. Since this is the only available date, we used these figures despite the shortcomings.

2. Anita N. Martinez was interviewed by Valerie Martinez-Ebers on April 27, 2004 (Martinez 2004). Additionally, Valerie Martinez-Ebers wishes to acknowledge José Angel Gutiérrez and the University of Texas at Arlington Special Collections for allowing the author to use the transcript of Dr. Gutiérrez's interview with Martinez (Martinez 1999).

3. Maria A. Berriozábal was interviewed by Sharon A. Navarro on February 2, 2004.

4. Graciela (Gracie) Saenz was interviewed by Irasema Coronado on June 14, 2004.

5. Consuelo Montalvo was interviewed by Sonia García on March 5, 2004.

6. Laredo information was obtained from the Laredo Chamber of Commerce <http://www.laredochamber.com/relocationinfo/facts/index.htm>.

7. "County Clerk Nominee Draws Opposition," *El Paso Times,* November 4, 1974.

8. "Vote Totals in El Paso County," *El Paso Times,* November 6, 1974.

9. "Expect Light Vote Turnout," *El Paso Times,* November 4, 1974.

10. Martinez 1999.

11. See "Mexican American Industrial Migrants," 1971.

12. Alicia Chacón was interviewed by Irasema Coronado on February 3, 2004.

13. Martinez 2004.

14. Montalvo 2004.

15. "Council Orders Airport Review," *Laredo Morning Times* <*http://madmax .lmtonline.com/textarchives/0817/s2.htm*>.

16. El Paso Inc. <*www.elpasoinc.com.archive/03-01-05/interview.html*>.

17. <http://aliciaChacón.yisd.net/>.

BIBLIOGRAPHY

Acker, Joan. 1990. "Hierarchies, Jobs, Bodies: A Theory of Gendered Organizations." *Gender and Society* 4 (2): 139–158.

Acosta, Teresa Palomo, and Ruthe Winegarten. 2003. *Las Tejanas: 300 Years of History.* Austin: University of Texas Press.

Acuña, Rudy. 1998. *Occupied America: A History of Chicanos.* New York: HarperCollins.

Ambrosius, Margery, and Susan Welch. 1984. "Women and Politics at the Grassroots: Women Candidates for State Office in Three States, 1950–1978." *The Social Science Journal* 21: 29–42.

American Bar Association. 1994. Report. Taskforce on Opportunities for Minorities. Chicago.

———. 2005a. "ABA Commission on Racial and Ethnic Diversity in the Profession." <www.abanet.org/minorities/mwan/burdens.html>.

———. 2005b. "ABA Commission on the Women in the Profession." <www.abanet.org/women/home.html>.

Anzaldúa, Gloria. 1987. *Borderlands/La Frontera: The New Mestiza.* San Francisco: Aunt Lute Books.

Baca Zinn, Maxine. 1980. "Gender and Ethnicity Among Chicanos." *Frontiers* 5: 18–23.

Baldez, Lisa. 2003. "Elected Bodies: The Gender Quota Law for Legislative Candidates in Mexico." Paper presented at the annual meeting of the American Political Science Association, Philadelphia, Pennsylvania, August 28–31.

Barrera Bassols, Dalia, and Alejandra Massolo. 1998. *Mujeres que gobiernan municipios: Experiencias, aportes y retos.* Mexico City: Colegio de México Programa Interdisciplinario de Estudios de la Mujer.

Barrett, Edith J. 1997. "Gender and Race in the State House: The Legislative Experience." *Social Science Journal* 34: 131–144.

————. 2001. "Black Women in State Legislatures: The Relationship of Race and Gender to the Legislative Experience." In *The Impact of Women in Public Office*, edited by Susan J. Carroll, 185–204. Bloomington: Indiana University Press.

Barvosa-Carter, Edwina. 2001. "Chicanas and Latinas (Re)Shaping Political Practice: Components of Chicana Strategies." Paper presented at the annual conference of the Western Political Science Association, Las Vegas, Nevada, March 14–17.

Bedolla, Lisa Garcia, Katherine Tate, and Janelle Wong. 2005. "Indelible Effects: The Impact of Women of Color in the U.S. Congress." In *Women and Elective Office*, edited by Sue Thomas and Clyde Wilcox, 152–175. New York: Oxford University Press.

Berriozábal, Maria. 2004. Interview by Sharon A. Navarro, February 2.

Black, Gordon S. 1972. "A Theory of Political Ambition: Career Choices and the Role of Structural Incentives." *American Political Science Review* 66: 144–159.

Bledsoe, Timothy, and Mary Herring. 1990. "Victims of Circumstances: Women in Pursuit of Political Office." *American Political Science Review* 84: 213–223.

Boles, Janet. 1984. "The Texas Women in Politics: Role Model or Mirage?" *The Social Science Journal* 21: 79–89.

Booth, Brittney. 2003a. "Vela Makes Her Mark." *Brownsville Herald*, May 5, pp. A1, A11.

————. 2003b. "Mayor Won't Seek Re-election." *Brownsville Herald*, May 21, pp. A1, A12.

Brown, Lyle, Joyce Langenegger, Sonia García, and Ted Lewis. 2003. *Practicing Texas Politics*. 12th ed. Boston: Houghton Mifflin.

Brown, Lyle, Bob Trotter, Joyce Langenegger, and Sonia García. 2001. *Practicing Texas Politics*. 11th ed. Boston: Houghton Mifflin.

Burka, Paul. 1989. "The Best and the Worst Legislators." *Texas Monthly* (July). Austin: Texas Monthly, Inc.

Burrell, Barbara. 1990. "The Presence of Women Candidates and the Role of Gender in Campaigns for the State Legislature in an Urban Setting." *Women and Politics* 3: 85–102.

————. 2003. "Money and Women's Candidacies for Public Office." In *Women and American Politics: New Questions, New Directions*, edited by Susan Carroll. New York: Oxford University Press.

Burt-Way, Barbara, and Rita Mae Kelly. 1992. "Gender and Sustaining Political Ambition: A Study of Arizona Elected Officials." *Western Political Quarterly* 45 (1): 11–26.

Camp, Roderic A. 1979. "Women and Political Leadership in Mexico: A Comparative Study of Female and Male Political Elites." *Journal of Politics* 41 (1) (May): 417–441.

————. 2002. *Politics in Mexico: The Democratic Transition*. 4th ed. Oxford: Oxford University Press.

Canter, Dorothy, Toni Bernay, and Jean Stoess. 1992. *Women in Power: The Secrets of Leadership*. Boston: Houghton Mifflin.

Cardenas, Maria de la Luz Rodríguez. 1998. "Laredo Women in Politics: Fearless Voices in a Common Struggle." In *Las Tejanas: 300 Years of History* (2003), edited by Teresa Palomo Acosta and Ruthe Winegarten. Austin: University of Texas Press.

Carroll, Susan. 1994. *Women as Candidates in American Politics*. 2nd ed. Bloomington: Indiana University Press.

———, editor. 2001. *The Impact of Women in Public Office*. Bloomington: Indiana University Press.

———. 2004. "Representing Women: Congresswomen's Perceptions of Their Representational Roles." In *Women Transforming Congress*, edited by Cindy S. Rosenthal, 50–68. Norman: University of Oklahoma Press.

Carroll, Susan, and Richard Fox, editors. 2005. *Gender and Elections: Shaping the Future of American Politics*. Cambridge: Cambridge University Press.

Center for American Women and Politics. 1999. "Women State Legislators: Leadership Position and Committee Chairs, Fact Sheet." Rutgers University, New Brunswick, New Jersey.

———. 2001. "Women Elected Office by State, Fact Sheet." Rutgers University, New Brunswick, New Jersey.

———. 2005. "Women in State Legislatures, Facts and Findings." Rutgers University, New Brunswick, New Jersey <www.rci.Rutgers.edu/~cawp>.

———. N.d. "Elección Latina." <www.rci.Rutgers.edu/~cawp/Eleccion/home.htm>.

Center for Mexican American Studies, University of Texas–Arlington. "Tejano Voices Interviewees." Oral History Project. <http://libraries.uta.edu/tejanovoices>.

Chacón, Alicia. 2004. Interview by Irasema Coronado, February 3.

———. 2005. "Alicia Chacón." Interview. <www.elpasoinc.com.archive/03 01 03/interview.html>.

Chandler, Davidson. 1990. *Race and Class in Texas Politics*. Princeton, New Jersey: Princeton University Press.

Chaney, Elsa. 1979. *Supermadre: Women in Politics in Latin America*. Austin: University of Texas Press.

Clark, Janet. 1998. "Women at the National Level: An Update on Roll Call Voting Behavior." In *Elective Office: Past, Present, and Future*, edited by Sue Thomas and C. Wilcox, 118–129. Oxford: Oxford University Press.

Clark, Janet, R. Darcy, Susan Welch, and Margery Ambrosius. 1984a. "Women as Legislative Candidates in Six States." In *Political Women: Current Roles in State and Local Government*, edited by Janet Flammang. Beverly Hills, California: Sage.

———. 1984b. "Women in State and Local Politics: Progress or Stalemate?" *Social Science Journal* 21: 1–4.

Cohen, Cathy, Kathleen Jones, and Joan Tronto, editors. 1997. *Women Transforming Politics*. New York: New York University Press.

"Conference Examines Women in Public Life." 1975. *The Record. LBJ Livewire Weekly Edition—Time Capsule* <www.lbjlivewire.com/content.php?content.19>.

Conover, Pamela Johnson, and Virginia Gray. 1983. "Feminism and the New Right: Conflict Over the American Family." New York: Praeger.

Conway, M. Margaret, Gertrude A. Steurnagle, and David W. Ahern. 1997. "Women and Political Participation." Washington, D.C.: Congressional Quarterly Press.

Córdova, Teresa, Norma Cantú, Gilberto Cardenas, Juan García, and Christine M. Sierra, editors. 1986. *Chicana Voices: Intersections of Class, Race, and Gender.* Albuquerque: University of New Mexico Press.

Cotera, Martha. 1976. *Diosa y Hembra: The History and Heritage of Chicanas in the U.S.* Austin: Information Systems Development.

Crenshaw, Kimberle. 1989. "Demarginalizing the Intersection of Race and Sex: A Black Feminist Critique of Antidiscrimination Doctrine, Feminist Theory, and Antiracist Politics." In *University of Chicago Legal Forum*, 139–167. Chicago: University of Chicago.

————. 1997. "Beyond Racism and Misogyny: Black Feminism and 2 Live Crew." In *Women Transforming Politics*, edited by Cathy Cohen, Kathy Jones, and Joan Tronto. New York: New York University Press.

Danini, Carmina. 2003. "Irma Rangel, 1931–2003, Longtime South Texas Legislator Dies." *San Antonio Express-News*, March 19, p. A3.

Darcy, Robert, Margaret Brewer, and Judy Clay. 1984. "Women in the Oklahoma Political System: State Legislative Elections." *Social Science Journal* 21: 67–78.

Darcy, Robert, Susan Welch and Janet Clark. 1994. *Women, Elections, and Representation.* New York: Longman.

————. 1996. "Women in the State Legislative Power Structure: Committee Chairs." *Social Science Quarterly* 77: 888–898.

Darling, Marsha J. 1998. "African-American Women in State Elective Office in the South." In *Women and Elective Office*, edited by Sue Thomas and Clyde Wilcox. New York: Oxford University Press.

Davidson, Chandler. 1990. *Race and Class in Texas Politics.* Princeton, New Jersey: Princeton University Press.

DeLeon, Arnoldo. 1993. *Mexican Americans in Texas: A Brief History.* 2nd ed. Wheeling, Illinois: Harlan Davidson.

Diamond, Irene. 1977. *Sex Roles in the State House.* New Haven, Connecticut: Yale University Press.

Dolan, Kathleen, and Lynne Ford. 1997. "Change and Continuity Among Women State Legislators: Evidence From Three Decades." *Political Research Quarterly* 50 (1): 151–187.

Duerst-Lahti, Georgia. 1998. "The Bottleneck: Women Becoming Candidates." In *Women and Elective Office: Past, Present, and Future*, edited by Sue Thomas and Clyde Wilcox, 15–25. New York: Oxford University Press.

Duerst-Lahti, Georgia, and Rita Mae Kelly, editors. 1995. *Gender Power, Leadership, and Governance.* Ann Arbor: University of Michigan Press.

Elazar, Daniel. 1984. *American Federalism: A View from the States.* 3rd ed. New York: Harper and Row.

Ellickson, Mark, and Donald Whistler. 2000. "A Path Analysis of Legislative Success in Professional and Citizen Legislatures: A Gender Comparison." *Women and Politics* 21 (4): 77–103.

Fikac, Peggy. 2003. "Farewell to Rangel." *San Antonio Express-News,* March 22, p. B1.

Flammang, Janet. 1984. *Political Women: Current Roles in State and Local Government.* Beverly Hills, California: Sage Publications.

Flores, Elizabeth. 2004. Interview by Sonia García, January 8.

Fowlkes, Diane. 1984. "Ambitious Political Women: Counter-socialization and Political Party Context." *Women and Politics* 4: 5–32.

Fox, Richard L. 2004. "Entering the Arena? Gender and the Decision to Run for Office." *American Journal of Political Science* 48: 264–280.

Fox, Richard, and Jennifer L. Lawless. 2003. "Family and Structure, Sex-Role Socialization, and the Decision to Run for Office." *Women and Politics* 24: 19–48.

Fox, Richard, Jennifer L. Lawless, and Courtney Feeley. 2001. "Gender and the Decision to Run for Office." *Legislative Studies Quarterly* 26: 411–435.

Fraga, Luis Ricardo, V. Martinez-Ebers, L. Lopez, and R. Ramirez. 2005. "Strategic Intersectionality: Gender, Ethnicity, and Political Incorporation." Paper presented at the annual meeting of the Western Political Science Association, Oakland, California, March 17–19.

Fraga, Luis Ricardo, V. Martinez-Ebers, R. Ramirez, and L. Lopez. 2001. "Gender and Ethnicity: The Political Incorporation of Latina and Latino State Legislators." Paper presented at the annual meeting of the American Political Science Association, San Francisco, California, August 30–September 2.

Fraga, Luis Ricardo, and Sharon A. Navarro. 2004. "Latinas in Latino Politics." Paper presented at the Conference on Latino Politics: The State of the Discipline, Texas A&M University, College Station, April 29.

Franks, Jeff. 1987. "Mizzoner?" *San Antonio Monthly* (March): 25–29, 64–66. <www.trial.com/Blogger/2001_11_01_Trial-BlogArchive.htm>.

Gaddie, R. K., and Charles Bullock. 1995. "Congressional Elections and the Year of the Woman: Structural and Elite Influences on Female Candidacies." *Social Science Quarterly* 76: 749–762.

García, Alma. 1989. "The Development of Chicana Feminist Discourse." *Gender and Society* 3: 217–238.

García, Alma, and Mario T. García, editors. 1997. *Chicana Feminist Thought: The Basic Historical Writings.* New York: Routledge.

García, Domingo. 2000. Interview by Valerie Martinez-Ebers, Dallas, July 13.

García, John A. 2003. *Latino Politics in America: Community, Culture, and Interests.* Lanham, Maryland: Rowman and Littlefield.

García, Sonia R. 1997a. "Empowering Women: San Antonio Style." Panel presentation at the annual conference of the Social Science Association, San Antonio, Texas, March 13–15.

―――. 1997b. "Motivational Factors for Latinas in Electoral Politics." Paper presented at the annual conference of the Western Political Science Association, Tucson, Arizona, March 13–15.

―――. 1998. "Running as a Latina: Building a Campaign." Paper presented at the annual meeting of the Western Political Science Association, Los Angeles, March 19–21.

―――. 2001. "Texas Women: Leadership Roles Among Women State Legislators in the 1990s." Paper presented at the annual meeting of the Western Political Science Association, Las Vegas, Nevada, March 15–17.

García, Sonia, and Laura Berberena. 2004. "Gender, Ethnicity and Context: Dynamics in a Texas Congressional Primary Race." Working paper.

García, Sonia, and Marisela Márquez. 1992. "Political Ambition and Aspirations Among Latinas." Roundtable on Latinas in Politics. Presented at the annual conference of the National Association for Chicano Studies, San Antonio, Texas, March 25–28.

―――. 2001. "Motivational and Attitudinal Factors Amongst Latinas in U.S. Electoral Politics." National Women's Studies Association Journal 13 (2): 112–122.

―――. 2005. "Mobilizing Change: An Examination of Latina Political Organizations." Paper presented at the annual conference of the Western Political Science Association, Oakland, California, March 16–19.

George, Alexander L., and Andrew Bennett. 2005. Case Studies and Theory Development in the Social Sciences. Cambridge: MIT Press.

Gomez, Lisa Marie. 1999. "Border City Elects Woman." San Antonio Express-News, May 3, p. 1A.

Gomez-Quiñones, Juan. 1990. Chicano Politics: Reality and Promise, 1940–1990 (The Calvin P. Horn Lectures in Western History and Culture). Albuquerque: University of New Mexico Press.

Green, Joanne Connor. 2003. "The Times . . . Are They A-Changing? An Examination of the Impact of the Value of Campaign Resources for Women and Men Candidates for the U.S. House of Representatives." Women and Politics 25: 1–29.

Greer, Jim. 2001. "Law Spawns New Hispanic Bank in Houston." Houston Business Journal, November 7. <http://houston.bizjournals.com>.

Gruberg, Martin. 1984. "From Nowhere to Where? Women in State and Local Politics." Social Science Journal 21: 5–12.

Guerra, Fernando. 1991. "The Emergence of Ethnic Officeholders in California." In Racial and Ethnic Politics in California, edited by Bryan Jackson and Michael Preston. Berkeley: University of California, Berkeley Institute of Governmental Studies.

Guerrero, Lena. 2004. Interview by Patricia Jaramillo, February 14.

Gutiérrez, José Angel. 1998. The Making of a Chicano Militant. Madison: University of Wisconsin Press.

Gutiérrez, José Angel, and Rebecca E. Deen. 2000. "Chicanas in Texas Politics." JSRI Occasional Paper 66. East Lansing, Michigan: Julian Samora Institute, Michigan State University.

Gutiérrez, José Angel, Michelle Melendez, and Sonia A. Noyola. 2006. *Chicanas in Charge: Texas Women in the Electoral Arena.* Lanham, Maryland: Altamira Press.

Hair, Penda. 2001. *Louder Than Words: Lawyers, Communities, and the Struggle for Justice.* New York: Rockefeller Foundation.

Hardy-Fanta, Carol. 1993. *Latina Politics, Latino Politics: Gender, Culture, and Political Participation in Boston.* Boston: Temple Press.

———. 1997. "Latina Women and Political Consciousness: La chispa que prende." In *Women Transforming Politics: An Alternative Reader,* edited by Cathy Cohen, Kathleen Jones, and Joan Tronto, 223–237. New York: New York Press.

Hawkesworth, Mary. 2003. "Congressional Enactments of Race-Gender: Toward a Theory of Raced-Gendered Institutions." *American Political Science Review* 97 (4): 529–550.

Hernández, Antonia. 1976. "Chicanas and the Issue of Involuntary Sterilization: Reforms Needed to Protect Informed Consent." *Chicano Law Review* 3: 3–37.

Hero, Rodney. 1998. *The Faces of Inequality: Social Diversity in American Politics.* New York: Oxford University Press.

Holley, Danielle, and Delia Spencer. 1999. "The Texas Ten Percent Plan." *Harvard Civil Liberties–Civil Rights Law Review* 34: 245–253.

Hoppe, Christy. 1991. "Lena Guerrero: A Railroad Commissioner Who's on the Fast Track." *Dallas Morning News,* September 1, p. E1.

———. 1992a. "Poll Shows Guerrero Leading Slightly in Race for Rail Panel." *Dallas Morning News,* September 6, p. A34.

———. 1992b. "Guerrero Admits She Never Received Degree." *Dallas Morning News,* September 12, p. A1.

———. 1992c. "Guerrero Says Claim Was Error." *Dallas Morning News,* September 14, p. B17.

———. 1992d. "Guerrero Says She Won't Open College Records." *Dallas Morning News,* September 15, p. A1.

Hotchkin, Sheila. 2005. "Perry's Judicial Nod Earns Applause." *San Antonio Express-News,* April 3, p. B1.

Hurtado, Aida. 1996. *The Color of Privilege: Three Blasphemies on Race and Feminism.* Ann Arbor: University of Michigan Press.

Hurwitz, Mark, and Drew Lanier. 2003. "Explaining Judicial Diversity: The Differential Ability of Women and Minorities to Attain Seats on State Supreme Court and Appellate Courts." *State Politics and Policy Quarterly* 3 (4): 329–352.

Institute for Women's Policy Research <www.iwpr.org>. 1996. "The Status of Women in Texas." Washington, D.C.: Institute for Women's Policy Research.

Jackson, Bryan, and Michael Preston, editors. 1991. *Racial and Ethnic Politics in California.* Berkeley: University of California Institute of Governmental Studies.

Jacobson, Gary. 1987. "The Marginals Never Vanished: Incumbency and Competition in Elections to the U.S. House of Representatives." *American Journal of Political Science* 31: 126–141.

Jeydel, Alana, and Andrew J. Taylor. 2003. "Are Women Legislators Less Effective? Evidence from the U.S. House in the 103rd–105th Congress." *Political Research Quarterly* 56 (1): 19–27.

Jones, Nancy Baker, and Ruthe Winegarten. 2000. *Capitol Women: Texas Female Legislators, 1923–1999.* Austin: University of Texas Press.

Kahn, Kim Fridkin. 1993. "Gender Differences in Campaign Messages: The Political Advertisement of Men and Women Candidates for the U.S. Senate." *Political Research Quarterly* 46: 481–501.

Kanter, Rosabeth. 1977. "Some Effects of Proportion on Group Life: Skewed Sex Ratios and Response to Token Women." *American Journal of Sociology* 82: 965–990.

Kapar, Vatsula. 1998. "Women's Contribution to the Democratization of Mexican Politics: An Exploration of Their Formal Participation in the National Action Party and the Party of the Democratic Revolution." *Mexican Studies/Estudios Mexicanos* 14 (2) (summer): 363–388.

Kathlene, Lyn. 1989. "Uncovering the Political Impacts of Gender: An Exploratory Study." *Western Political Quarterly* 42 (2): 397–421.

———. 1994. "Power and Influence in State Legislative Policymaking: The Interaction of Gender and Position in Committee Hearing Debates." *American Political Science Review* 88 (3): 560–576.

Kazee, Thomas A. 1994. *Who Runs for Congress? Ambition, Context, and Candidate Emergence.* Washington, D.C.: CQ Press.

Kenney, Sally J. 1996. "New Research on Gendered Political Institutions." *Political Research Quarterly* 49 (2): 445–466.

Kirkpatrick, Jeane. 1974. *Political Women.* New York: Basic Books.

Kraemer, Richard H., Charldean Newell, and David F. Prindle. 2001. *Essentials of Texas Politics.* 8th ed. Belmont, California: Wadsworth.

La Cour Dabelko, Kristen, and Paul Herrnson. 1997. "Women and Men's Campaigns for the U.S. House of Representatives." *Political Research Quarterly* 50: 121–135.

Laredo, City of. 2003. Office of the Mayor. "Biography of Betty Flores." <www.cityoflaredo.com/mayor-council/MayorBio2003%20.htm>. Accessed on August 24, 2004.

———. 2004. "Presidential Kudos for Laredo Mayor." Press release. <www.cityoflaredo.com/citynews/07-14-04Presidential Kudos for Laredo Mayor.htm>. Accessed July 14, 2005.

Laredo Chamber of Commerce. 2004. "Facts of Laredo." <www.laredochamber.com/relocationinfo/facts/index.html>.

Lawless, Jennifer, and Richard Fox. 2005. *It Takes a Candidate: Why Women Don't Run for Office.* Cambridge: Cambridge University Press.

Legislative Reference Library of Texas. 2007. "Membership Statistics." <www.lrl.state.tx.us>.

Leo, Myra. 2003. "It Was Always About the Students." *The Texas Observer* 95 (7) (April 11). <www.texasobserver.org.Archives>.

———. 2005. Telephone interview by Valerie Martinez-Ebers, April 30.

López, Alma. 2004. Interview by Sonia R. García, January 5.

Magaña, Lisa. 2005. *Mexican Americans and the Politics of Diversity: Querer es Poder.* Tucson: University of Arizona Press.

Mansbridge, Jane. 1999. "Should Blacks Represent Blacks, and Women Represent Women? A Contingent 'Yes.'" *The Journal of Politics* 61: 628–657.

Márquez, Ben. 2003. "One Dream, Many Voices: The Mexican American Women's National Association." In *Constructing Identities in Mexican American Political Organizations: Crossing Issues, Taking Sides,* 91–111. Austin: University of Texas Press.

Márquez, Marisela. 1997. "Redefining Politics: Survey on Chicano and Latina Political Actors." Paper presented at the annual conference of the Western Political Science Association, Tucson, Arizona, March 13–15.

Martin, Elaine, and Barry Pyle. 2002. "Gender and Racial Diversification of State Supreme Courts." *Women and Politics* 24 (2): 35–52.

Martinez, Anita. 1999. "Oral History Interview with Anita Martinez, by José Angel Gutiérrez." CMAS No. 129. <http://libraries.uta.edu/tejanovoices/transcripts/TV_129.html>.

———. 2004. Interview by Valerie Martinez-Ebers, April 27.

Mason, Julie. 1997. "Contests for Mayor, Proposition A in Homestretch." *Houston Chronicle,* November 3, p. A1.

Massolo, Alejandra. 2002. "Tienen que luchar alcaldesas para legitimarse en el poder." <www.cimacnoticias.com/noticias/02jul/02071202.html>. Accessed December 12, 2003.

McGaffey, Edna. 1990. "Women On the Bench: A Conspicuous Absence of Hispanics." *San Antonio Express-News,* October 21, p. A1.

Melville, Margarita B., editor. 1980. *Twice a Minority: Mexican American Women.* St. Louis: C. V. Mosby.

"Mexican American Industrial Migrants." 1971. Institute of Urban Studies, Southern Methodist University. Mimeo provided by Anita Martinez.

Moncrief, Gary, Peverill Squire, and Malcolm Jewell. 2001. *Who Runs for the Legislature?* New York: Prentice Hall.

Montalvo, Consuelo (Chelo). 2004. Interview by Sonia García, March 5.

Montoya, Lisa, Carol Hardy-Fanta, and Sonia García. 2000. "Latina Politics: Gender, Participation, and Leadership." *PS: Political Science and Politics* 23 (3): 555–562.

Moreno, Sylvia. 2004. "Democrats Gaining a Foothold in Texas." *Washington Post,* November 10, p. A3.

Morris, Julie. 1991. "Texas Woman Breaking Down Old Barriers." *USA Today,* January 16.

Muñoz, Frances. 2002a. "Directory of Latino/a Federal Judges." *Berkeley La Raza Law Journal* 13: 95–101.

———. 2002b. "Overcoming Barriers: Being Flexible and Creative." *Berkeley La Raza Law Journal* 13: 29–32.

National Association of Latino Elected Officials (NALEO) <www.naleo.org>. 1985. *National Directory of Latino Elected Officials.* Washington, D.C.

————. 1995. *National Directory of Latino Elected Officials*. Washington, D.C.

————. 2005. *National Directory of Latino Elected Officials*. Washington, D.C.

Navarro, Armando. 1998. *The Cristal Experiment*. Madison: University of Wisconsin Press.

Navarro, Sharon A. 2002. "Las mujeres invisibles/The Invisible Women." In *Women's Activism and Globalization: Linking Local Struggles and Transnational Politics*, edited by Nancy Naples and Manisha Desai, 83–98. New York: Routledge.

Newman, Jody. 1994. "Perception and Reality: A Study Comparing the Success of Men and Women Candidates." Prepared for the National Women's Political Caucus, Washington, D.C.

Niven, David. 1998. "Party Elites and Women Candidates: The Shape of Bias." *Women and Politics* 19: 57–80.

Norton, Noelle. 1995. "Women, It's Not Enough to be Elected: Committee Position Makes a Difference." In *Gender Power, Leadership, and Governance*, edited by Georgia Duerst-Lahti and Rita Mae Kelly, 115–140. Ann Arbor: University of Michigan Press.

Ontiveros, Maria. 1993. "Three Perspectives on Workplace Harassment of Women of Color." *Golden Gate University Law Review* 23: 817–828.

Pachon, Harry, and Louis DeSipio. 1992. "Latino Elected Officials in the 1990s." *PS: Political Science and Politics* 25: 212–217.

Pardo, Mary. 1990. "Mexican American Grassroots Community Activists: 'Mothers of East Los Angeles.'" *Frontiers* 11 (1): 1–7.

————. 1998. *Mexican American Women Activists: Identity and Resistance in Two Los Angeles Communities*. Philadelphia: Temple University Press.

Pesquera, Beatriz, and Denise Segura. 1993. "There Is No Going Back: Chicanas and Feminism." In *Chicana Critical Issues*, edited by Norma Alarcón, Rafaela Castro, Emma Pérez, Beatriz Pesquera, Adaljiza Sosa Riddell, and Patricia Zavella, 95–116. Berkeley: Third Woman Press.

Poole, Keith T., and L. Harmon Zeigler. 1985. *Women, Public Opinion, and Politics: The Changing Political Attitudes of American Women*. New York: Longman.

Potter, Linda. 1998. "Women in the Texas Legislature: Seen and Heard? A Preliminary Study of Memberships and Chairships on Mega Committees." In *Texas Politics Today*, edited by William Maxwell and Ernest Crain, 145–148. Stamford, Connecticut: West/Wadsworth Publishing.

Prindeville, Diane M. 2002. "A Comparative Study of Native American and Hispanic Women in Grassroots and Electoral Politics." *Frontiers* 23 (1): 67–89.

Prindeville, Diane M., and John G. Bretting. 1998. "Indigenous Women Activists and Political Participation: The Case of Environmental Justice." *Women and Politics* 19 (1): 39–58.

————. 1999. "Identity and the Politics of Native and Mexican American Women Leaders." Paper presented at the annual conference of the Western Political Science Association, Seattle, March 24–27.

Rangel, Irma. 1996. Interview by José Angel Gutiérrez, Kingsville, Texas, April 10. University of Texas at Arlington Special Collections.

———. 2000. Telephone interview by Valerie Martinez-Ebers, May 23.

"A Resource Guide to Hispanic Women's Organizations." 1994. *Intercambios: A Publication of the National Network of Hispanic Women* 6 (2): i–vii.

Rodríguez, Victoria, editor. 1998. *Women's Participation in Mexican Political Life.* Boulder, Colorado: Westview Press.

———. 2003. *Women in Contemporary Mexican Politics.* Austin: University of Texas Press.

Roman, Mary. 2004. Interview by Sonia R. García, January 9.

Rosales, Rodolfo. 2000. *The Illusion of Inclusion: The Untold Story of San Antonio.* Austin: University of Texas Press.

Rosenthal, Cindy Simon. 1998. *When Women Lead.* New York: Oxford University Press.

———. 2000. "Gender Styles in State Legislative Committees: Raising Their Voices in Resolving Conflict." *Women and Politics* 21 (2): 21–45.

———, editor. 2004. *Women Transforming Congress.* Norman: University of Oklahoma Press.

Ruiz, Vicki L. 1998. *From Out of the Shadows: Mexican Women in Twentieth Century America.* New York: Oxford University Press.

Saenz, Graciela (Gracie). 2004. Interview by Irasema Coronado, June 14.

Saint-Germain, Michelle. 1989. "Does Their Difference Make a Difference? The Impact of Women on Public Policy in the Arizona State Legislature." *Social Science Quarterly* 70: 956–968.

Salinas Ender, Elma. 2004a. Interview by Sonia R. García, January 8.

———. 2004b. "341st District Court: Judge Salinas Ender Has Been Serving for Over 20 Years." *Laredo Morning Times,* January 25.

Sánchez Vela, Blanca. 2003. Interview by Sharon A. Navarro, October 27.

Sapiro, Virginia. 1983. *The Political Integration of Women: Roles, Socialization, and Politics.* Urbana: University of Illinois Press.

Sapiro, Virginia, and Barbara Farah. 1980. "New Pride and Old Prejudice: Political Ambition and Role Orientations Among Female Partisan Elites." *Women and Politics* 1: 13–37.

Schlesinger, Joseph. 1966. *Ambition and Politics: Political Careers in the United States.* Chicago: Rand McNally.

Segura, Denise A. 1986. "Chicanas and Triple Oppression in the Labor Force." In *Chicana Voices: Intersection of Class, Race, and Gender,* edited by Teresa Córdova, Norma Cantú, Gilberto Cardenas, Juan García, and Christine M. Sierra, 47–65. Albuquerque: University of New Mexico Press.

Serna, Diana. 2004. E-mail message to Sharon A. Navarro, August 20.

Serna, Olivia. 2004. Interview by Sharon A. Navarro, April 6.

Shockley, John. 1974. *Chicano Revolt in a Texas Town.* Notre Dame, Indiana: University of Notre Dame Press.

Siems, Larry. 1999. "Loretta Sanchez and the Virgin." *Aztlán: A Journal of Chicano Studies* 24 (1): 151–174.

Sierra, Christine M. 1997. "From Activist to Mayor: The Controversial Politics of Debbie Jaramillo in Santa Fe, New Mexico." Panel presentation at the annual meeting of the Western Political Science Association, Tucson, Arizona, March 13–15.

Sierra, Christine M., and Adaljiza Sosa-Riddell. 1994. "Chicanas as Political Actors: Rare Literature, Complex Practice." *National Political Science Review* 4: 297–317.

Smooth, Wendy G. 2001. "African American Women State Legislators: The Impact of Gender and Race on Legislative Influence." Ph.D. dissertation. University of Maryland, College Park.

Sotomayor, Sonia. 2002. "A Latina Judge's Voice. *Berkeley La Raza Law Journal* 13: 87–93.

Sparks, Holloway. 1997. "Dissident Citizenship: Democratic Theory, Political Courage, and Activist Women." *Hypatia* 12 (4): 74–110.

Squire, Peverill. 1992. "Legislative Professionalization and Membership Diversity in State Legislatures." *Legislative Studies Quarterly* 17: 69–79.

Stanley-Coleman, Jeanie R. 1996. "Gender Politics in the 1994 Texas Election." *Texas Journal of Political Studies* 18: 4–31.

Steinberg, Ronnie J. 1992. "Gender on the Agenda: Male Advantage in Organizations." *Contemporary Sociology* 21 (5): 576–581.

Stille, Alexander. 2001. "Prospecting for Truth in the Ore of Memory." *New York Times*, March 10, p. B9.

Stone, Walter J., and L. Sandy Maisel. 2003. "The Not-So-Simple Calculus of Winning: Potential U.S. House Candidates' Nomination and General Election Prospects." *Journal of Politics* 65: 955–971.

Swers, Michele, and Carin Larson. 2005. "Women in Congress: Do They Act as Advocates for Women's Issues?" In *Women and Elective Office: Past, Present, and Future,* edited by Sue Thomas and Clyde Wilcox, 412–444. New York: Oxford University Press.

Takash-Cruz, Paule. 1993. "Breaking Barriers to Representation: Chicana/Latina Elected Officials in California." *Urban Anthropology* 22: 325–360.

———. 1997. "Breaking Barriers to Representation: Chicana/Latina Elected Officials in California. Reprinted in *Women Transforming Politics: An Alternative Reader,* edited by Cathy Cohen, Kathleen Jones, and Joan Tronto, 412–434. New York: New York Press.

Tamerius, Karin L. 1995. "Sex, Gender, and Leadership in the Representation of Women." In *Gender Power, Leadership, and Governance,* edited by Georgia Duerst-Lahti and Rita Mae Kelly, 93–112. Ann Arbor: University of Michigan Press.

Texas Secretary of State, Elections Division. 2007. Election History, 1992–2007. <*http://elections.sos.state.tx.us/elchist.exe*>.

Texas State Historical Association. 2002. "Handbook of Texas Online: Mexican American Women." Austin: University of Texas. <*www.tsha.utexas.edu/handbook/online/articles/view/MM/pwmly.html*>.

Thomas, Sue. 1994. *How Women Legislate.* New York: Oxford University Press.

————. 1998. "Introduction: Women and Elective Office: Past, Present, and Future." In *Women and Elective Office*, edited by Sue Thomas and Clyde Wilcox, 1–14. New York: Oxford University Press.

Thomas, Sue, and Clyde Wilcox, editors. 1998. *Women and Elective Office: Past, Present, and Future.* New York: Oxford University Press.

————. 2005. *Women and Elective Office.* New York: Oxford University Press.

Thomas, Sue, and Susan Welch. 1991. "The Impact of Gender on Activities and Priorities of State Legislators." *Western Political Science Quarterly* 44 (2): 445–456.

Tolleson-Rinehart, Sue, and Jeanie R. Stanley. 1994. *Claytie and the Lady: Ann Richards, Gender, and Politics in Texas.* Austin: University of Texas Press.

Trager, Cara S. 1987. "Carving Out a Niche in Politics." *Hispanic Business* (October): 29–31.

Valencia, Reynaldo, Sonia R. García, Henry Flores, and Roberto Juárez. 2004. *Mexican Americans and the Law: El Pueblo Unido Jamás Será Vencido.* Tucson: University of Arizona Press.

Van de Putte, Leticia. 2004. Interview by Patricia Jaramillo, January 11.

Vega, Arturo. 1997. "Gender and Ethnicity Effects on the Legislative Behavior and Substantive Representation of the Texas Legislature." *Texas Journal of Political Studies* 19: 1–18.

Vega, Arturo, and Juanita Firestone. 1995. "The Effects of Gender on Congressional Behavior and the Substantive Representation of Women." *Legislative Studies Quarterly* 20: 213–222.

Vidal, Mirta. 1971. *Chicanas Speak Out! Women: New Voice of La Raza.* New York: Pathfinder Press.

Walsh, Katherine Cramer. 2002. "Enlarging Representation: Women Bringing Marginalized Perspectives to Floor Debate in the House of Representatives." In *Women Transforming Congress*, edited by Cindy S. Rosenthal, 370–398. Norman: University of Oklahoma Press.

Whitaker, Lois Duke. 2005. *Women in Politics: Outsiders or Insiders?* 4th ed. Upper Saddle River, New Jersey: Prentice Hall.

Witt, Linda, M. Paget, and Glenna Matthews. 1995. *Running as a Woman: Gender and Power in American Politics.* New York: Free Press.

Yañes, Linda. 2004. Interview by Sonia R. García, January 26.

Zaffirini, Judith. 2004. Interview by Patricia Jaramillo, March 22.

Zuniga, Leo. 2003. "State Rep. Irma Rangel Is Remembered." *ACCD Newsletter* (spring).

INDEX

CPSIA information can be obtained
at www.ICGtesting.com
Printed in the USA
FFHW021423040119
50053501-54881FF